French Favorite Kids Songs & Rhymes

A Mama Lisa Book

French Favorite Kids Songs & Rhymes - A Mama Lisa Book

Original Material Written by Lisa Yannucci

Translations by Monique Palomares and Lisa Yannucci

Additional Translations by Our Many Correspondents

Songs Selected by Monique Palomares

Compiled and Edited by Jason Pomerantz

Visit Mama Lisa on the web at www.MamaLisa.com

(c) 2012 by Lisa Yannucci

Contents

Introduction

Songs & Rhymes
1. À cheval sur mon bidet
(Riding My Horsey)

2. À déli délo
(Ah Deli Delo)

3. À la claire fontaine
(At the Clear Spring)

4. Ah ! Mon beau château !
(Oh! My Beautiful Castle!)

5. Ah ! Vous dirai-je Maman
(Oh! Shall I Tell You Mommy)

6. Alouette, gentille alouette
(Lark, Sweet Lark)

7. Au clair de la lune
(Under the Moonlight)

8. Au feu les pompiers
(Fire! Firemen, Fire!)

9. Aux marches du palais
(Down the Palace Stairs)

10. Bonjour Guillaume
(Good Morning, William)

11. C'est Gugusse
(It's Gugusse)

12. Cadet Rousselle

13. Compagnons de la Marjolaine
(Company of the Marjoram)

14. Compère Guilleri
(Fellow Guilleri)

15. Dans la forêt lointaine
(In the Faraway Forest)

16. Douce nuit
(Sweet Night)

17. Frère Jacques
(Brother John)

18. Gentil coquelicot
(Nice Poppy)

19. Il court le furet
(The Ferret Runs)

20. Il était un petit navire
(There Was a Little Ship)

21. Il était une bergère
(There Was a Shepherdess)

22. Il était un' dame Tartine
(There Was a Lady Slice of Bread)

23. J'ai du bon tabac
(I Have Good Tobacco)

24. J'ai perdu le do de ma clarinette
(I Lost the C on My Clarinet)

25. J'ai vu le loup, le renard, le lièvre
(I Saw the Wolf, The Fox, The Hare)

26. J'aime la galette
(I Love Cake)

27. Jean Petit qui danse
(John Petit)

28. La bonne aventure ô gué
(A Fine Adventure, Oh Joy!)

29. La légende de Saint Nicolas
(The Legend of Saint Nicholas)

30. La mère Michel
(Old Ma Michel)

31. Le bon roi Dagobert
(The Good King Dagobert)

32. Le carillon de Vendôme
(The Chimes of Vendôme)

33. Le coq est mort
(The Rooster Is Dead)

34. Le grand cerf
(The Big Deer)

35. Lundi matin
(On Monday Morning)

36. Malbrough s'en va-t-en guerre
(Marlborough Is Going to War)

37. Maudit sois-tu carillonneur
(Curse You Bell-ringer)

38. Meunier, tu dors
(Miller, You're Sleeping)

39. Mon âne
(My Donkey)

40. Mon beau sapin
(My Beautiful Fir Tree)

41. Nous n'irons plus au bois
(We'll Go to the Woods No More)

42. Pirouette cacahuète
(Pirouette Peanut Butter)

43. Pomme de reinette et pomme d'api
(Pippin Apple and Lady Apple)

44. Promenons-nous dans les bois
(Let's Stroll in the Woods)

45. Savez-vous planter les choux ?
(Do You Know How to Plant Cabbage?)

46. Sur le plancher une araignée
(A Spider on the Floor)

47. Sur le pont d'Avignon
(On the Bridge of Avignon)

48. Sur le pont du Nord
(On the North Bridge)

49. Trois jeunes tambours
(Three Young Drummers)

50. Trois petits chats
(Three Little Cats)

51. Un éléphant, ça trompe
(One Elephant That Deceives)

52. Un éléphant se balançait
(One Elephant was Swinging on a Spider Web)

53. Un kilomètre à pied ça use, ça use
(One Kilometer on Foot Wears Out Your Shoes for Good)

54. Un petit cochon
(A Little Pig)

55. Un, deux, trois, nous allons au bois
(One, Two, Three, We Are Going into the Woods)

56. Une poule sur un mur
(A Hen on a Wall)

57. Une souris verte
(A Green Mouse)

58. Vent frais, vent du matin
(Fresh Wind, Morning Wind)

Thanks and Acknowledgements

About Us

Introduction

France! Home of Paris and Provence. Land of amazing food and the Eiffel Tower. Host to much of the world's best art. Endowed with a rich tradition of children's songs and rhymes.

In this book we've gathered over 50 of France's best-loved traditional children's songs, presented in their original French language and with translations into English. Many have commentary sent to us by our correspondents who are immersed in the traditions and culture of France.

You'll find well-known songs like FRÈRE JACQUES (Brother John), ALOUETTE, GENTILLE ALOUETTE (Lark, Sweet Lark) and AU CLAIR DE LA LUNE (Under the Moon), alongside many you may never have heard of.

These songs are still sung today, but many hark back to France's rich history. A time when church bells were still used to tell the time, as in FRÈRE JACQUES. A romantic time when knights roamed the land looking for love, as in COMPAGNONS DE LA MARJOLAINE (Company of the Marjoram).

If you're not a native you'll have a chance to learn the songs that every French child knows and loves.

At Mama Lisa's World we work with ordinary people around the globe to build a platform to preserve and exchange traditional culture. Most of the songs and rhymes featured here have been provided by our contributors, to whom we're very grateful! (Please see the Thanks and Acknowledgements section for a complete list of everyone who has contributed.) We love to receive new (public domain) material, so if one of your favorites has not been included please visit our website and write us to let us know.

The material presented here is part of a living tradition. So the version of a song you know may have some different words. Tell us about it! We consider our collection a dialogue and we update it all the time with your comments.

At the end of each item in this book, there's a web address to an online version of the song or rhyme. There we are often able to include sheet music, recordings and videos of performances.

We hope this book will help foster a love of French songs and culture all over the world!

Merci!

Mama Lisa
(Lisa Yannucci)
www.mamalisa.com

Songs and Rhymes

1

À cheval sur mon bidet (Riding My Horsey)

À cheval sur mon bidet
(French Children's Song)

À cheval sur mon bidet* (1)
Quand il trotte, il est parfait
Au pas, au pas, au pas, (2)
Au trot, au trot, au trot (3)
Au galop, au galop, au galop ! (4)

Riding My Horsey
(English Translation)

Riding my horsey,
When he trots, he is perfect,
At a walk, at a walk, at a walk,
At a trot, at a trot, at a trot,
At a gallop, at a gallop, at a gallop.

Notes

*A "bidet" was small horse from Brittany used as a draft horse. The breed is now extinct.

There are several variations of this song. Here are some line by line:

1st Line: *Riding on a horse in French is "à cheval" (literally "on horse"). Baby talk for "horse" is "coco" or "dada", so the line can start with "à coco" or "à dada". In this case, the line would be either, "À dada sur mon bidet" or "À coco sur mon bidet".*

"Bidet" is sometimes "baudet" (donkey) instead.

2nd Line: *This line can be "Quand il marche, il fait des pets"(When he walks he farts).*

3rd Line: *This line can be in the same scatological shade as the previous one:*

"Quand il trotte, il fait des crottes" (When he trots he makes some droppings).

4th Line: *The last line can be: "Quand il galope, au galop, au galop, au galop" (When he gallops, at a gallop, at a gallop, at a gallop).*

Stéphane Jourdan wrote: "It seems to me that the song ends (at least in my family) after the "galop" with: 'Tombé dans la rivière' (Fallen into the river): While the adult spreads her legs, the child falls but is held by the hands and also gets hooked on the knees (the adult holds him/her tightly by the hands)."

You will find **"Sur le cheval de Grand-papa"** *(http://www.mamalisa.com/?t=es&p=2884&c=22) as a variant to this song.*

Game Instructions

(1) Sit the child on your lap, holding his hands and make him bounce as if riding a horse.

(2) Make a slow beat with your legs.

(3) Speed up the rhythm.

(4) End with a gallop!

For more about À cheval sur mon bidet, go to:
http://www.mamalisa.com/?t=es&p=2905.

There, you'll find sheet music, an MP3 tune and a MIDI melody.

2

À déli délo (Ah Deli Delo)

This is a hand-clapping rhyme. The game instructions are below the song.

À déli délo
(French Hand Clapping Rhyme)

A déli déli déli délo.
Partons pour Chicago - cago
Ce sera rigolo - golo
Pour draguer les minettes - minettes
Qui jouent avec leurs couettes
Bigoudi bigouda, caramel au chocolat.

Le lendemain matin - matin
Je me suis réveillé(e) - veillé(é)
À cause d'un petit bébé - areu areu
Qui ne voulait pas manger – berk
Sa soupe préférée – miam miam.

Ma mère est boulangère – hmmmmmmm
Mon père est policier –
Passez mesdames,
Passez messieurs, stop, prison
Ma sœur est une Indienne – ouh ouh ouh ouh
Mon frère est un cow-boy –
Dring dring, pan pan, tchick-a-tchick han han
Et moi je suis un petit cochon
En forme de queue en tire-bouchon – bou

Si j'avais une petite sœur
Je l'appellerais Sophie
Si j'avais un petit frère
Je l'appellerais Napoléon...

Ah Deli Delo
(English Translation)

Ah deli deli deli delo,
Let's start for Chicago - cago,
That will be funny - ny,
To try to pick up chicks – chicks,
Who play with their pigtails,
Curly curlate, caramel with chocolate.

The next morning – morning,
I woke up – woke up,
Because of a little baby – goo-goo,
Who didn't want to eat – yuck -
His favorite soup – yum, yum.

My mother is a baker – yummmmmmm,
My father is a policeman –
Pass by ladies,
Pass by gentlemen, stop, prison,
My sister is an Indian – ooh ooh ooh ooh
My brother is a cowboy –
Ring-ring, bang-bang, chick-a-chick-a hee-haw,
And I am a little pig
In the shape of a corkscrew-shaped tail - boo!

If I had a little sister,
I'd call her Sophia,
If I had a little brother,
I'd call him Napoleon...

Notes

Monique said, "This is a literal translation. This rhyme is based on a much older one ("À véli vélo" = "On a bicy – bicycle" that would be totally politically incorrect by now). It has been changing with time and has reached this present form, but I suppose that other versions are sung in French school playgrounds."

Game Instructions

-1st take your left elbow with your right hand, then hold your partner's right elbow with your left hand. Your partner should do the same. Then swing this "square" gently from right to left while singing, "À déli, déli déli délo".

-The handclapping is as follows:

Clap your hands.
Then, left hand facing down, right hand facing up, clap your partner's hands. Your partner does the same.
Reverse movement.
Clap your partner's hands at shoulder height.

-Keep going and insert the following movements on the following lyrics:

Minettes: Turn your hair around your forefinger.
Bigoudi, bigouda, caramel et chocolat: Same movement.
Matin: Stretch your arms (as if waking up).
Réveillée: Rub your eyes with your fists.
Areu areu: Rub your eyes with your fists.
Berk: Pretend to push away a plate with your hands.
Manger: Rub your stomach.
Passez mesdames, passez messieurs, stop, prison: Wave your right hand from right to left as a policemen would do to allow people to pass. Then wave it the other way around with your left hand. Then bring your hand from the shoulder to waist as if chopping to mean "stop".
Dring, dring: Use your earlobe to pretend you're ringing a bicycle bell.
Pan pan: Pretend you're shooting.
Chick a chick han han: Move your shoulders as if you were riding a horse.
Queue en tire bouchon: Make a corkscrew gesture with your finger at the bottom of your back.

For more about À déli délo, go to: **http://www.mamalisa.com/?t=es&p=1439**.

There, you'll find an MP3 tune.

À la claire fontaine (At the Clear Spring)

The word "fontaine" can refer to a fountain or a natural spring. In this song it's referring to a spring.

À la claire fontaine
(French Children's Song)

À la claire fontaine,
M'en allant promener
J'ai trouvé l'eau si belle
Que je m'y suis baigné

Refrain :
Il y a longtemps que je t'aime
Jamais je ne t'oublierai

Sous les feuilles d'un chêne,
Je me suis fait sécher
Sur la plus haute branche,
Un rossignol chantait

Refrain

Chante rossignol, chante,
Toi qui as le cœur gai
Tu as le cœur à rire,
Moi je l'ai à pleurer

Refrain

J'ai perdu mon amie,
Sans l'avoir mérité
Pour un bouquet de roses,
Que je lui refusai.

Refrain

Je voudrais que la rose,
Fût encore au rosier
Et que ma douce amie
Fût encore à m'aimer.*

Refrain

At the Clear Spring
(English Translation)

At the clear spring,
As I was strolling by,
I found the water so nice
That I went in to bathe.

(Chorus)
It's so long I've been loving you,
That I'll never forget you.

Under an oak tree,
I dried myself.
On the highest branch
A nightingale was singing.

(Chorus)

Sing, nightingale, sing,
Your heart is so happy.
Your heart feels like laughing,
Mine feels like weeping.

(Chorus)

I lost my beloved
Without deserving it
Over a bouquet of roses
That I refused to give her.

(Chorus)

I wanted the rose
To stay on the rosebush,
And for my sweet love
To be still loving me.

(Chorus)

Notes

There's another version of the last 2 lines:

ET QUE LE ROSIER MÊME
À LA MER FÛT JETÉ.

(AND THAT THE ROSEBUSH
BE THROWN INTO THE SEA.)

Photos & Illustrations

Comments

There's a **Quebecoise** *(http://www.mamalisa.com/?t=es&p=346&c=51) and a Creole version of this song.*

For more about À la claire fontaine, go to:
http://www.mamalisa.com/?t=es&p=141.

There, you'll find sheet music, an MP3 tune, a MIDI melody and a video performance.

Ah ! Mon beau château ! (Oh! My Beautiful Castle!)

This is normally a girls circle game. The girls make two circles, one smaller than the other, then the two circles turn in opposite directions. The smaller circle sings the first verse and then the larger circle answers with the next verse.

Ah ! Mon beau château !
(French Circle Game Song)

Première ronde :
Ah ! Mon beau château !
Ma tant', tire, lire, lire ;
Ah ! Mon beau château !
Ma tant', tire, lire, lo.

Deuxième ronde :
Le nôtre est plus beau,
Ma tant', tire, lire, lire ;
Le nôtre est plus beau,
Ma tant', tire, lire, lo.

Première ronde :

Nous le détruirons,
Ma tant', tire, lire, lire ;
Nous le détruirons,
Ma tant', tire, lire, lo.

Deuxième ronde :
Comment ferez-vous ?
Ma tant', tire, lire, lire ;
Comment ferez-vous ?
Ma tant', tire, lire, lo.

Première ronde :
Nous prendrons vos filles.
Ma tant', tire, lire, lire ;
Nous prendrons vos filles
Ma tant', tire, lire, lo.

Deuxième ronde :
Laquell' prendrez-vous,
Ma tant', tire, lire, lire ;
Laquell' prendrez-vous,
Ma tant', tire, lire, lo ?

Première ronde :
Celle que voici,
Ma tant', tire, lire, lire ;
Celle que voici,
Ma tant', tire, lire, lo.

Deuxième ronde :
Que lui donn'rez-vous,
Ma tant', tire, lire, lire ;
Que lui donn'rez-vous,
Ma tant', tire, lire, lo ?

Première ronde :
De jolis bijoux,
Ma tant', tire, lire, lire ;
De jolis bijoux,
Ma tant', tire, lire, lo.

Deuxième ronde :
Nous n'en voulons pas,
Ma tant', tire, lire, lire ;
Nous n'en voulons pas,
Ma tant', tire, lire, lo.

Oh! My Beautiful Castle!
(English Translation)

First Circle:
Oh! My beautiful castle!

My aunt, tier, leer, leer*.
Oh! My beautiful castle!
My aunt, tier, leer, lo.

Second Circle:
Ours is more beautiful,
My aunt, tier, leer, leer.
Ours is more beautiful,
My aunt, tier, leer, lo.

First Circle:
We will destroy it,
My aunt, tier, leer, leer.
Ours is more beautiful,
My aunt, tier, leer, lo.

Second Circle:
How will you do that?
My aunt, tier, leer, leer.
How will you do that?
My aunt, tier, leer, lo.

First Circle:
We will take your girls
My aunt, tier, leer, leer;
We will take your girls
My aunt, tier, leer, lo.

Second Circle:
Which one will you take?
My aunt, tier, leer, leer;
Which one will you take?
My aunt, tier, leer, lo.

First Circle:
We will take this one,
My aunt, tier, leer, leer;
We will take this one
My aunt, tier, leer, lo.

Second Circle:
What will you give her?
My aunt, tier, leer, leer;
What will you give her?
My aunt, tier, leer, lo.

First Circle:
Some beautiful jewels,
My aunt, tier, leer, leer;
Some beautiful jewels,
My aunt, tier, leer, lo.

Second Circle:
We don't want any,

My aunt, tier, leer, leer;
We don't want any,
My aunt, tier, leer, lo.

Notes

*Translated for the sound of the words. Literally it means, "My aunt, pull, read, read" but it's really meaningless.

I found this version which makes more sense:

Ah mon beau château !
Ma tatan, vire, vire, vire,
Ah mon beau château !
Ma tatan, vire, vire beau.

Translation:

Oh my beautiful castle!
My Auntie, turns, turns, turns,
Oh my beautiful castle!
My Auntie, turns, turns beautifully.

Source: "Chansons populaires de l'Ain" by Charles Guillon (1883)

*****

In some versions there are more verses between the 3rd and 4th verse that go:

À coups de canons… (With cannon shots).

Ou à coups de bâtons… (With whacks of a stick).

Nous le referons… (We'll make it again).

Encor' bien plus beau… (Even more beautiful).

Game Instructions

After the smaller circle offers beautiful jewels and they're turned down, they go on offering other things (beautiful shoes, etc…) until the bigger circle answers, "Nous en voulons bien" ("We will accept them"). Then the girl chosen as "this one" leaves the bigger circle to join the smaller one. The game goes on until the circle that started out as the largest one has only two or three girls left, and thus it has become the smaller one and then the game starts again.

For more about Ah ! Mon beau château !, go to:
http://www.mamalisa.com/?t=es&p=2257.

There, you'll find sheet music, an MP3 tune and a MIDI melody.

Ah ! Vous dirai-je Maman (Oh! Shall I Tell You Mommy)

Ah ! Vous dirai-je Maman
(French Children's Song)

Ah ! Vous dirai-je Maman
Ce qui cause mon tourment ?
Papa veut que je raisonne
Comme une grande personne
Moi je dis que les bonbons
Valent mieux que la raison.

Oh! Shall I Tell You Mommy
(English Translation)

Oh! Shall I tell you, Mommy
What is tormenting me?
Daddy wants me to reason
Like a grown-up person,
Me, I say that sweets
Are worth more than reasoning.

For more about Ah ! Vous dirai-je Maman, go to:
http://www.mamalisa.com/?t=es&p=143.

There, you'll find sheet music, an MP3 tune, a MIDI melody and a video performance.

Alouette, gentille alouette (Lark, Sweet Lark)

The song ALOUETTE, GENTILLE ALOUETTE *is about plucking a lark to cook and eat. In the old days this was common.*

Alouette, gentille alouette
(French Children's Song)

Refrain
Alouette, gentille alouette,
Alouette, je te plumerai.

Je te plumerai le bec,
Je te plumerai le bec,
Et le bec, et le bec,
Alouette, Alouette !
Ah ! ah ! ah ! ah !

(refrain)

Je te plumerai les yeux,
Je te plumerai les yeux,
Et les yeux, et les yeux,
Et le bec, et le bec,
Alouette, Alouette !
Ah ! ah ! ah ! ah !

(refrain)

Je te plumerai la tête,
Je te plumerai la tête
Et la tête, et la tête
Et les yeux, et les yeux,
Et le bec, et le bec,
Alouette, Alouette !
Ah ! ah ! ah ! ah !

(refrain)

Je te plumerai le cou,
Je te plumerai le cou,
Et le cou, et le cou,
Et la tête, et la tête
Et les yeux, et les yeux,
Et le bec, et le bec,
Alouette, Alouette !
Ah ! ah ! ah ! ah !

(refrain)

Je te plumerai le dos,
Je te plumerai le dos,
Et le dos, et le dos,
Et le cou, et le cou,
Et la tête, et la tête
Et les yeux, et les yeux,
Et le bec, et le bec,
Alouette, Alouette !
Ah ! ah ! ah ! ah !

(refrain)

Je te plumerai les ailes
Je te plumerai les ailes,
Et les ailes, et les ailes,
Et le dos, et le dos,
Et le cou, et le cou,
Et la tête, et la tête
Et les yeux, et les yeux,
Et le bec, et le bec,
Alouette, Alouette !
Ah ! ah ! ah ! ah !

(Refrain)

Je te plumerai le ventre,
Je te plumerai le ventre,
Et le ventre, et le ventre,
Et les ailes, et les ailes,
Et le dos, et le dos,
Et le cou, et le cou,

Et la tête, et la tête
Et les yeux, et les yeux,
Et le bec, et le bec,
Alouette, Alouette !
Ah ! ah ! ah ! ah !

(Refrain)

Je te plumerai les pattes,
Je te plumerai les pattes,
Et les pattes, et les pattes,
Et le ventre, et le ventre,
Et les ailes, et les ailes,
Et le dos, et le dos,
Et le cou, et le cou,
Et la tête, et la tête
Et les yeux, et les yeux,
Et le bec, et le bec,
Alouette, Alouette !
Ah ! ah ! ah ! ah !

(Refrain)

Je te plumerai la queue,
Je te plumerai la queue,
Et la queue, et la queue,
Et les pattes, et les pattes,
Et le ventre, et le ventre,
Et les ailes, et les ailes,
Et le dos, et le dos,
Et le cou, et le cou,
Et la tête, et la tête
Et les yeux, et les yeux,
Et le bec, et le bec,
Alouette, Alouette !
Ah ! ah ! ah ! ah !

(Refrain)

Lark, Sweet Lark
(English Translation)

(Chorus)
Lark, sweet lark,
Lark, I will pluck you.

I will pluck your beak,
I will pluck your beak
And your beak, and your beak,
Lark, lark, lark, lark.
Oh! Oh! Oh! Oh!

(Chorus)

I will pluck your eyes,
I will pluck your eyes
And your eyes, and your eyes,
And your beak, and your beak,
Lark, lark, lark, lark.
Oh! Oh! Oh! Oh!

(Chorus)

I will pluck your head,
I will pluck your head
And your head, and your head,
And your eyes, and your eyes
And your beak, and your beak
Lark, lark, lark, lark.
Oh! Oh! Oh! Oh!

(Chorus)

I will pluck your neck,
I will pluck your neck
And your neck, and your neck,
And your head, and your head,
And your eyes, and your eyes
And your beak, and your beak
Lark, lark, lark, lark.
Oh! Oh! Oh! Oh!

(Chorus)

I will pluck your back,
I will pluck your back
And your back, and your back,
And your neck, and your neck,
And your head, and your head,
And your eyes, and your eyes
And your beak, and your beak
Lark, lark, lark, lark.
Oh! Oh! Oh! Oh!

(Chorus)

I will pluck your wings,
I will pluck your wings,
And your wings, and your wings,
And your back, and your back,
And your neck, and your neck,
And your head, and your head,
And your eyes, and your eyes
And your beak, and your beak
Lark, lark, lark, lark.
Oh! Oh! Oh! Oh!

(Chorus)

I will pluck your belly,
I will pluck your belly,
And your belly, and your belly,
And your wings, and your wings,
And your back, and your back,
And your neck, and your neck,
And your head, and your head,
And your eyes, and your eyes
And your beak, and your beak
Lark, lark, lark, lark.
Oh! Oh! Oh! Oh!

(Chorus)

I will pluck your legs,
I will pluck your legs,
And your legs, and your legs,
And your belly, and your belly,
And your wings, and your wings,
And your back, and your back,
And your neck, and your neck,
And your head, and your head,
And your eyes, and your eyes
And your beak, and your beak
Lark, lark, lark, lark.
Oh! Oh! Oh! Oh!

(Chorus)

I will pluck your tail,
I will pluck your tail,
And your tail, and your tail,
And your legs, and your legs,
And your belly, and your belly,
And your wings, and your wings,
And your back, and your back,
And your neck, and your neck,
And your head, and your head,
And your eyes, and your eyes
And your beak, and your beak
Lark, lark, lark, lark.
Oh! Oh! Oh! Oh!

(Chorus)

Notes

We believe "Alouette" is originally from the French speaking part of Canada, but it's very popular in France.

Comments

Come visit MAMA LISA'S WORLD BLOG *to learn about* **the meaning of the song Alouette** *(http://www.mamalisa.com/blog/alouette-is-not-a-mean-song-really/).*

For more about Alouette, gentille alouette, go to:
http://www.mamalisa.com/?t=es&p=1446.

There, you'll find sheet music, an MP3 tune and a MIDI melody.

Au clair de la lune (Under the Moonlight)

Au clair de la lune
(French Children's Song)

Au clair de la lune
Mon ami Pierrot
Prête-moi ta plume*
Pour écrire un mot
Ma chandelle est morte
Je n'ai plus de feu
Ouvre-moi ta porte

Pour l'amour de Dieu

Au clair de la lune
Pierrot répondit
Je n'ai pas de plume
Je suis dans mon lit
Va chez la voisine
Je crois qu'elle y est
Car dans sa cuisine
On bat le briquet

Au clair de la lune
L'aimable Lubin
Frappe chez la brune
Qui répond soudain
Qui frapp' de la sorte
Il dit à son tour
Ouvrez votre porte
Au dieu de l'amour

Au clair de la lune
On n'y voit qu'un peu
On chercha la plume
On chercha du feu
En cherchant d' la sorte
Je n' sais c' qu'on trouva
Mais je sais qu' la porte
Sur eux se ferma.

Under the Moonlight
(English Translation)

Under the moonlight:
"My friend Pierrot
Lend me your pen
So I can write a note.
My candle is out,
I no longer have a light.
Open your door for me,
For the love of God!"

Under the moonlight:
Pierrot replied,
"I don't have a pen,
I'm in my bed.
Go to the neighbor's house,
I believe she's there,
Because in her kitchen,
Someone lit a match."

Under the moonlight:
Kind Rubin

Knocks at the brunette's door.
All of a sudden she replies,
"Who's knocking like that?"
He says in turn,
"Open your door,
For the god of love."

Under the moonlight:
Only a little can be seen,
The pen was looked for
A light was looked for,
Searching like this
I don't know what was found,
But I do know that the door
Was closed on them.

Notes

Re. plume (pen): The original version in Old French went, "Prête-moi ta lume" meaning "Lend me your light". As the years went by, LUME *(light) became* PLUME *(pen).*

Jean-Baptiste Lully (1632-1687) is thought to be the musical composer of this song.

Photos & Illustrations

Comments

If you'd like to listen to a more old-fashioned version, **here you can hear a 1931 recording of Au clair de la lune by Yvonne Printemps** *(http://gauterdo.com/ref/aa/au.clair.de.la.lune.html).*

For more about Au clair de la lune, go to:
http://www.mamalisa.com/?t=es&p=161.

There, you'll find sheet music, an MP3 tune, a MIDI melody and a video performance.

Au feu les pompiers (Fire! Firemen, Fire!)

Au feu les pompiers
(French Children's Song)

Au feu, les pompiers !
La maison qui brûle,
Au feu, les pompiers !
La maison brûlée.

C'est pas moi qui l'ai brûlée,
C'est la cuisinière*,
C'est pas moi qui l'ai brûlée,
C'est le cuisinier*.

Au feu, les pompiers !
La maison qui brûle,
Au feu, les pompiers !
La maison brûlée.

Fire! Firemen, Fire!
(English Translation)

Fire! Firemen, fire!
The house is burning.
Fire! Firemen, fire!
The house burnt down.

It's not me who burnt it down,
It's Miss Chef*,
It's not me who burnt it down,
It's Mr. Chef*.

Fire! Firemen, fire!
The house is burning.
Fire! Firemen, fire!
The house burnt down.

Notes

In French, these words mean "the cook". First it's a female cook (cuisinière), then a male cook (cuisinier). Since we don't have a perfect way to indicate that it's feminine or masculine in English, we translated it as Miss Chef and Mr. Chef. An older version of the song had the term as "la cantinière" (the female canteen cook) and "le cantinier" (the male canteen cook). Monique wrote, "I don't know what the origin is, but I think it might be a military song. The term 'la cantinière' was used in the military, there was no 'canteen' anywhere else. Also, the tune sounds like a clarion call."

Comments

Monique said, "The version I know goes like the one below, the third verse is sung to the same tune as the first verse…"

Au feu, les pompiers !
La maison qui brûle.
Au feu, les pompiers !
La maison est brûlée.

Ce n'est pas moi qui l'ai brûlée,
C'est mon frère Jules,
Ce n'est pas moi qui l'ai brûlée,
C'est mon frère André.

André, gare à toi,
Les gendarmes arrivent,
André, gare à toi,
Les gendarmes sont là !

Translation

Fire! Firemen, Fire!
The house is burning.

Fire! Firemen, Fire!
The house is burnt.

It's not me who burned it,
It's my brother Jules,
It's not me who burned it,
It's my brother Andrew.

Andrew, watch out,
The police are coming,
Andrew, watch out,
The police are here.

For more about Au feu les pompiers, go to:
http://www.mamalisa.com/?t=es&p=2916.

There, you'll find sheet music, an MP3 tune and a MIDI melody.

Aux marches du palais (Down the Palace Stairs)

Aux marches du palais
(French Children's Song)

Aux marches du palais
Aux marches du palais
Y a une tant belle fille, lon la,
Y a une tant belle fille.

Elle a tant d'amoureux,
Elle a tant d'amoureux
Qu'elle ne sait lequel prendre, lon la,
Qu'elle ne sait lequel prendre.

C'est un p'tit cordonnier,

C'est un p'tit cordonnier,
Qui eu sa préférence, lon la,
Qui eu sa préférence.

Et c'est en la chaussant,
Et c'est en la chaussant,
Qu'il lui fit sa demande, lon la,
Qu'il lui fit sa demande.

La belle si tu voulais,
La belle si tu voulais,
Nous dormirions ensemble, lon la,
Nous dormirions ensemble.

Dans un grand lit carré,
Dans un grand lit carré,
Couvert de toile blanche, lon la,
Couvert de toile blanche.

Aux quatre coins du lit,
Aux quatre coins du lit,
Un bouquet de pervenches*, lon la,
Un bouquet de pervenches.

Dans le mitan du lit,
Dans le mitan du lit,
La rivière est profonde, lon la,
La rivière est profonde.

Tous les chevaux du roi,
Tous les chevaux du roi,
Pourraient y boire ensemble, lon la,
Pourraient y boire ensemble.

Nous y serions heureux,
Nous y serions heureux,
Jusqu'à la fin du monde, lon la,
Jusqu'à la fin du monde.

Down the Palace Stairs
(English Translation)

Down the palace stairs,
Down the palace stairs,
There is such a pretty girl, lon la,
There is such a pretty girl...

She has so many suitors,
She has so many suitors,
That she doesn't know which to choose, lon la,
That she doesn't know which to choose...

It's the little shoemaker,
It's the little shoemaker,
That she prefers, lon la,
That she prefers...

While he put shoes on her,
While he put shoes on her,
He proposed to her, lon la,
He proposed to her...

Pretty one, if you'd like,
Pretty one, if you'd like,
We could sleep together, lon la,
We could sleep together...

In a large square bed,
In a large square bed,
Covered with a white cloth, lon la,
Covered with a white cloth...

At the four corners of the bed,
At the four corners of the bed,
A bouquet of periwinkles*, lon la,
A bouquet of periwinkles...

In the middle of the bed,
In the middle of the bed,
The river is so deep, lon la,
The river is so deep...

That all the king's horses,
That all the king's horses
Could drink there together, lon la,
Could drink there together...

We would be happy there,
We would be happy there
Until the end of the world, lon la,
Until the end of the world.

Notes

An alternate for line is: "Le rossignol y chante" ("The nightingale sings there.")

For more about Aux marches du palais, go to:
http://www.mamalisa.com/?t=es&p=3559.

There, you'll find an MP3 tune and a MIDI melody.

Bonjour Guillaume (Good Morning, William)

BONJOUR GUILLAUME *is a circle game. You can learn how to play it below…*

Bonjour Guillaume
(French Circle Game Song)

Bonjour Guillaume
As-tu bien déjeuné?
Oh oui madame,
J'ai mange du pâté,
Du pâté d'alouette,
Guillaume et Guillaumette,
Chacun s'embrassera,
Guillaume restera.

Good Morning, William
(English Translation)

Good morning William,
Did you have a good breakfast?
Oh, yes, madam,
I had some paté,
Lark paté,
William and Wilma,
Everyone hugs each other,
William will be left alone.

Notes

Here's a "singable" translation:

Good morning, William,
Was your breakfast good?
Yes indeed, madam,
Pâté was very good,
Pâté made with skylark,
William and Wilma Clark,
Everyone finds their friend,
William's alone again.

Game Instructions

You need an odd number of players to play this game. The children hold hands and form a circle. One child goes in the center, s/he is "William". The children walk around in a circle and sing. At the end of the song, the children hug each other two by two. The one remaining alone is the next "William" and the game starts all over again.

For more about Bonjour Guillaume, go to:
http://www.mamalisa.com/?t=es&p=2230.

There, you'll find sheet music, a MIDI melody and a video performance.

C'est Gugusse (It's Gugusse)

C'est Gugusse
(French Children's Song)

C'est Gugusse avec son violon
Qui fait danser les filles
Qui fait danser les filles
C'est Gugusse avec son violon
Qui fait danser les filles et les garçons.
Mon papa ne veut pas que je danse, que je danse
Mon papa ne veut pas que je danse la polka
Il dira ce qu'il voudra*, moi je danse moi je danse
Il dira ce qu'il voudra, moi je danse la polka du roi.

It's Gugusse
(English Translation)

It's Gugusse with his violin
Who makes the girls go a-dancing,
Who makes the girls go a-dancing.
It's Gugusse with his violin
Who makes the girls and the boys go a-dancing.
My dad doesn't want me to dance, me to dance
My dad doesn't want me to dance the polka.
He will say what he wants, still I'll dance, still I'll dance,
He will say what he wants, still I'll dance the king's polka.

Notes

The last 2 lines can be sung this way:

Mais quand il n'y est pas, moi je danse, moi je danse,
Mais quand il n'y est pas, moi je danse la polka.

English Translation:

But when he's not here, I dance, I dance,
But when he's not here, I dance the polka.

Some people add "du roi" at the end of the last line, some don't. If you do add it, then it's "je danse la polka du roi" (I dance the king's polka).

For more about C'est Gugusse, go to: **http://www.mamalisa.com/?t=es&p=2920**.

There, you'll find sheet music, an MP3 tune, a MIDI melody and a video performance.

Cadet Rousselle

Cadet Rousselle was an actual person who lived from 1743 - 1807. He was a French bailiff who went to jail for a short time. He was an eccentric person and he even made his house a bit eccentric. This song satirizes him.

Cadet Rousselle
(French Children's Song)

Cadet Rousselle a trois maisons,
Cadet Rousselle a trois maisons,
Qui n'ont ni poutres, ni chevrons,
Qui n'ont ni poutres, ni chevrons,
C'est pour loger les hirondelles,
Que direz-vous d' Cadet Rousselle ?

Ah ! Ah ! Ah ! oui vraiment,
Cadet Rousselle est bon enfant.

Cadet Rousselle à trois habits,
Cadet Rousselle à trois habits,
Deux jaunes, l'autre en papier gris,
Deux jaunes, l'autre en papier gris,
Il met celui-là quand il gèle,
Ou quand il pleut, ou quand il grêle.
Ah ! Ah ! Ah ! oui vraiment,
Cadet Rousselle est bon enfant.

Cadet Rousselle a trois beaux yeux,
Cadet Rousselle a trois beaux yeux,
L'un r'garde à Caen, l'autre à Bayeux,
L'un r'garde à Caen, l'autre à Bayeux,
Comme il n'a pas la vue bien nette,
Le troisième, c'est sa lorgnette.
Ah ! Ah ! Ah ! oui vraiment,
Cadet Rousselle est bon enfant.

Cadet Rousselle a une épée,
Cadet Rousselle a une épée,
Très longue, mais toute rouillée,
Très longue, mais toute rouillée,
On dit qu'ell' ne cherche querelle,
Qu'aux moineaux et qu'aux hirondelles.
Ah ! Ah ! Ah ! oui vraiment,
Cadet Rousselle est bon enfant.

Cadet Rousselle a trois garçons,
Cadet Rousselle a trois garçons,
L'un est voleur, l'autre est fripon,
L'un est voleur, l'autre est fripon,
Le troisième est un peu ficelle,
Il ressemble à Cadet Rousselle.
Ah ! Ah ! Ah ! oui vraiment,
Cadet Rousselle est bon enfant.

Cadet Rousselle a trois gros chiens,
Cadet Rousselle a trois gros chiens,
L'un court au lièvr', l'autre au lapin
L'un court au lièvr', l'autre au lapin,
L' troisièm' s'enfuit quand on l'appelle,
Comm' le chien de Jean d'Nivelle.
Ah ! Ah ! Ah ! oui vraiment,
Cadet Rousselle est bon enfant.

Cadet Rousselle à trois beaux chats,
Cadet Rousselle à trois beaux chats,
Qui n'attrapent jamais les rats,
Qui n'attrapent jamais les rats,
Le troisièm' n'a pas de prunelles,
Il monte au grenier sans chandelle.

Ah ! Ah ! Ah ! oui vraiment,
Cadet Rousselle est bon enfant.

Cadet Rousselle a marié,
Cadet Rousselle a marié,
Ses trois filles dans trois quartiers,
Ses trois filles dans trois quartiers,
Les deux premièr's ne sont pas belles,
La troisièm' n'a pas de cervelle.
Ah ! Ah ! Ah ! oui vraiment,
Cadet Rousselle est bon enfant.

Cadet Rousselle a trois deniers,
Cadet Rousselle a trois deniers,
C'est pour payer ses créanciers,
C'est pour payer ses créanciers,
Quand il a montré ses ressources,
Il les resserre dans sa bourse.
Ah ! Ah ! Ah ! oui vraiment,
Cadet Rousselle est bon enfant.

Cadet Rousselle ne mourra pas,
Cadet Rousselle ne mourra pas,
Car avant de sauter le pas,
Car avant de sauter le pas,
On dit qu'il apprend l'orthographe,
Pour fair' lui-mêm' son épitaphe.
Ah ! Ah ! Ah ! oui vraiment,
Cadet Rousselle est bon enfant.

Cadet Rousselle
(English Translation)

Cadet Rousselle has three houses,
Cadet Rousselle has three houses,
That have no beams or rafters,
That have no beams or rafters,
They give lodging to the swallows,
What will you say about Cadet Rousselle?
Oh! Oh! Oh! Yes indeed,
Cadet Rousselle is a good kid.

Cadet Rousselle has three suits,
Cadet Rousselle has three suits,
Two of them yellow, the other made out of grey paper,
Two of them yellow, the other made out of grey paper,
He wears the latter when it's freezing,
Or when it's raining or when it's hailing.
Oh! Oh! Oh! Yes indeed,
Cadet Rousselle is a good kid.

Cadet Rousselle has three beautiful eyes,

Cadet Rousselle has three beautiful eyes,
One looks at Caen, the other at Bayeux,
One looks at Caen, the other at Bayeux,
Since he has poor eyesight,
The third one is his spy-glass.
Oh! Oh! Oh! Yes indeed,
Cadet Rousselle is a good kid.

Cadet Rousselle has a sword,
Cadet Rousselle has a sword,
Very long, but all rusty,
Very long, but all rusty,
They say it only fights
Against sparrows and swallows.
Oh! Oh! Oh! Yes indeed,
Cadet Rousselle is a good kid.

Cadet Rousselle has three boys,
Cadet Rousselle has three boys,
One is a thief, the other is a knave,
One is a thief, the other is a knave,
The third one is somewhat crafty,
He looks like Cadet Rousselle.
Oh! Oh! Oh! Yes indeed,
Cadet Rousselle is a good kid.

Cadet Rousselle has three big dogs,
Cadet Rousselle has three big dogs,
One chases hares, the other rabbits,
One chases hares, the other rabbits,
The third one runs away when called,
Like Jean de Nivelle's dog.
Oh! Oh! Oh! Yes indeed,
Cadet Rousselle is a good kid.

Cadet Rousselle has three big cats,
Cadet Rousselle has three big cats,
One that never chases rats,
One that never chases rats,
The third one has no eyes,
It goes up to the attic without a candle.
Oh! Oh! Oh! Yes indeed,
Cadet Rousselle is a good kid.

Cadet Rousselle married off
Cadet Rousselle married off
His three daughters in three neighborhoods,
His three daughters in three neighborhoods.
The first two are not pretty,
The third one has no brains.
Oh! Oh! Oh! Yes indeed,
Cadet Rousselle is a good kid.

Cadet Rousselle has three pennies,

Cadet Rousselle has three pennies.
They're to pay his creditors,
They're to pay his creditors.
When he showed his money,
He put it back in his purse.
Oh! Oh! Oh! Yes indeed,
Cadet Rousselle is a good kid.

Cadet Rousselle will not die,
Cadet Rousselle will not die
Because before taking the plunge,
Because before taking the plunge,
They say he's learning how to spell,
To write his epitaph himself.
Oh! Oh! Oh! Yes indeed,
Cadet Rousselle is a good kid.

Notes

In 1792, Gaspard de Chenu, a satirical songwriter, wrote this song.

Photos & Illustrations

For more about Cadet Rousselle, go to:
http://www.mamalisa.com/?t=es&p=3539.

There, you'll find sheet music, a MIDI melody and a video performance.

Compagnons de la Marjolaine (Company of the Marjoram)

This song dates back to around 1650. It takes place in Paris.

Compagnons de la Marjolaine
(French Children's Song)

Qu'est-ce qui passe ici si tard ?
Compagnons de la Marjolaine,
Qu'est-ce qui passe ici si tard ?
Gai, gai, dessus le quai.

C'est le chevalier du guet,
Compagnons de la Marjolaine,
C'est le chevalier du guet,

Gai, gai, dessus le quai.

Que demande le chevalier ?
Compagnons de la Marjolaine,
Que demande le chevalier ?
Gai, gai, dessus le quai.

Une fille à marier,
Compagnons de la Marjolaine,
Une fille à marier,
Gai, gai, dessus le quai.

N'y a pas d' fille à marier,
Compagnons de la Marjolaine,
N'y a pas d' fille à marier,
Gai, gai, dessus le quai.

On m'a dit qu' vous en aviez,
Compagnons de la Marjolaine,
On m'a dit qu' vous en aviez,
Gai, gai, dessus le quai.

Ceux qui l'ont dit s' sont trompés,
Compagnons de la Marjolaine,
Ceux qui l'ont dit s' sont trompés,
Gai, gai, dessus le quai.

Je veux que vous m'en donniez,
Compagnons de la Marjolaine,
Je veux que vous m'en donniez,
Gai, gai, dessus le quai.

Sur les onze heur's repassez
Compagnons de la Marjolaine,
Sur les onze heur's repassez
Gai, gai, dessus le quai.

Les onze heur's sont bien passées,
Compagnons de la Marjolaine,
Les onze heur's sont bien passées,
Gai, gai, dessus le quai.

Sur les minuit revenez,
Compagnons de la Marjolaine,
Sur les minuit revenez,
Gai, gai, dessus le quai.

Les minuit sont bien sonnés,
Compagnons de la Marjolaine,
Les minuit sont bien sonnés,
Gai, gai, dessus le quai.

Mais nos filles sont couchées,
Compagnons de la Marjolaine,

Mais nos filles sont couchées,
Gai, gai, dessus le quai.

En est-il un' d'éveillée ?
Compagnons de la Marjolaine,
En est-il un' d'éveillée ?
Gai, gai, dessus le quai.

Qu'est-ce que vous lui donnerez ?
Compagnons de la Marjolaine,
Qu'est-ce que vous lui donnerez ?
Gai, gai, dessus le quai.

De l'or, des bijoux assez,
Compagnons de la Marjolaine,
De l'or, des bijoux assez,
Gai, gai, dessus le quai.

Ell' n'est pas intéressée,
Compagnons de la Marjolaine,
Ell' n'est pas intéressée,
Gai, gai, dessus le quai.

Mon cœur je lui donnerai,
Compagnons de la Marjolaine,
Mon cœur je lui donnerai,
Gai, gai, dessus le quai.

Dans ce cas-là choisissez,
Compagnons de la Marjolaine,
Dans ce cas-là choisissez,
Gai, gai, dessus le quai.

Company of the Marjoram
(English Translation)

"Who is passing by so late?
Company of the Marjoram
Who is passing by so late?
Hey! Hey! Over the quay!"

"It's the Knight Captain of the Watch,
Company of the Marjoram
It's the Knight Captain of the Watch,
Hey! Hey! Over the quay!"

"What is the Knight asking for?
Company of the Marjoram
What is the Knight asking for?
Hey! Hey! Over the quay!"

"A girl to marry,

Company of the Marjoram
A girl to marry,
Hey! Hey! Over the quay!"

"There aren't any girls here to marry,
Company of the Marjoram,
There aren't any girls here to marry,
Hey! Hey! Over the quay!"

They told me that you had some,
Company of the Marjoram,
They told me that you had some,
Hey! Hey! Over the quay!"

"Those who said so, they were wrong,
Company of the Marjoram,
Those who said so, they were wrong,
Hey! Hey! Over the quay!"

"I want you to find me some,
Company of the Marjoram,
I want you to find me some,
Hey! Hey! Over the quay!"

"Pass by again at eleven o'clock,
Company of the Marjoram,
Pass by again at eleven o'clock,
Hey! Hey! Over the quay!"

"Eleven o'clock has well passed,
Company of the Marjoram,
Eleven o'clock has well passed,
Hey! Hey! Over the quay!"

"Come back at midnight
Company of the Marjoram,
Come back at midnight
Hey! Hey! Over the quay!"

"Midnight has already struck,
Company of the Marjoram,
Midnight has already struck,
Hey! Hey! Over the quay!"

But our girls are all asleep,
Company of the Marjoram,
But our girls are all asleep,
Hey! Hey! Over the quay!"

"Is there one who is awake?
Company of the Marjoram,
Is there one who is awake?
Hey! Hey! Over the quay!"

"What will you give to her?
Company of the Marjoram,
What will you give to her?
Hey! Hey! Over the quay!"

"Plenty of gold and jewels,
Company of the Marjoram,
A lot of gold and jewels,
Hey! Hey! Over the quay!"

"She is not interested,
Company of the Marjoram,
She is not interested,
Hey! Hey! Over the quay!"

"I will give her my heart,
Company of the Marjoram,
I will give her my heart,
Hey! Hey! Over the quay!"

"In that case, make your choice,
Company of the Marjoram,
In that case, make your choice,
Hey! Hey! Over the quay!"

Notes

Note about the 1st Line:

The first line "Qu'est-ce qui passe ici si tard ? " translates literally to "What is passing by so late?" Another version of the 1st line is: "Qu'est-ce qui s' passe ici si tard" (What is happening here so late?) as you can hear in our mp3. Yet another version is "Qui est-ce qui passe ici si tard" (Who is passing by so late?).

Note about the meaning of the term "Compagnons de la Marjolaine":

Monique wrote: "Looking for information on the phrase, 'compagnons de la marjolaine', I came across a couple of websites. One explained that marjoram used to be used in love songs just like the rose or the lily of the valley. The other site explained how young men going out partying would put some sprigs of marjoram sticking out of the top of their boots. Hence forming an informal 'Fellowship of the Marjoram'. Both sites said that these men were 'charmers'.

The book, 'Trésors des plus belles mélodies de tous les temps et de tous les pays' (Delfolie, Editions Edsco, Chambéry, 1947) states that in the 15th century people wouldn't say 'to serenade someone'. Instead they would say, 'to wake up the pots of marjoram'.

The Brotherhood of the Marjoram (Confrérie de la Marjolaine) was the guild of perfumers. It was a very powerful guild because the king's court, and certain people in the city -good society I suppose- made very intense use of perfumes.

According to Du Mersan (Chants et chansons populaires de France, t. 2), the phrase 'compagnons de la marjolaine' was 'the meeting of young men and girls who go to dance in the meadow where the marjoram blooms'.

To sum it up, it seems that they were jolly good fellows!"

Note about the translation of the phrase "Compagnons de la Marjolaine":

"Compagnons de la Marjolaine" translates literally to "Companions of the Marjoram". Monique and I went back and forth for a good week discussing what would be the best way to translate it into English to make it understandable to today's audience. The meaning is close to "Fellowship of the Marjoram" or "Fellows of the Marjoram". "Company of the Marjoram" has a similar meaning to "Fellowship of the Marjoram", but it keeps the sound of the French "Compagnons de la Marjolaine" that's such an important part of the song. That's why we finally chose to translate it this way.

-Mama Lisa, January 2011

Note about the Translation of the term "Chevalier du guet":

A "Chevalier du guet" was a knight, and a nobleman, who was part of the city Watch. It's important to note that he was also the Captain of the Watch.

We had a hard time determining a translation of it into English that would get the meaning across.

Here's what Monique wrote about the meaning, "About 'Le chevalier du guet'... The historical fact is that he wasn't an ordinary Captain of the Watch. He was the Captain of the Paris watch and a nobleman -to use 'watchman' would make him an ordinary watchman which he wasn't. This guy was very important, he could go and find the king without being announced at any time...

I think that your suggestion "Knight Captain of the Watch" sounds good because you keep both meaning of knight and police officer included in 'le chevalier du guet'."

For more about Compagnons de la Marjolaine, go to:
http://www.mamalisa.com/?t=es&p=2997.

There, you'll find sheet music, an MP3 tune and a MIDI melody.

Compère Guilleri (Fellow Guilleri)

Compère Guilleri
(French Children's Song)

Il était un p'tit homme
Qui s'appelait Guilleri, carabi
Il s'en fut à la chasse
À la chasse aux perdrix, carabi

Refrain:
Titi, carabi, toto, carabo *,compère Guilleri
te laisseras-tu, te laiss'ras-tu, te laiss'ras-tu mouri**?

Il s'en fut à la chasse
À la chasse aux perdrix, carabi

Il monta sur un arbre
Pour voir ses chiens couri**, carabi

Refrain

Il monta sur un arbre
Pour voir ses chiens couri**, carabi
La branche vint à rompre
Et Guilleri tombit***, carabi

Refrain

La branche vint à rompre
Et Guilleri tombit***, carabi
Il se cassa la jambe
Et le bras se démit, carabi

Refrain

Il se cassa la jambe
Et le bras se démit, carabi
Les dam's de l'hôpital
Sont arrivées au bruit, carabi

Refrain

Les dam's de l'hôpital
Sont arrivées au bruit, carabi
L'une apporte un emplâtre
L'autre de la charpie, carabi

Refrain

L'une apporte un emplâtre
L'autre de la charpie, carabi
On lui banda la jambe
Et le bras lui remit, carabi

Refrain

On lui banda la jambe
Et le bras lui remit, carabi
Pour remercier ces dames
Guill'ri les embrassit***, carabi

Refrain

Pour remercier ces dames
Guill'ri les embrassit***, carabi
De cette belle histoire
La morale la voici, carabi

Refrain

De cette belle histoire
La morale la voici, carabi
Elle prouve que par les femmes
L'homme est toujours guéri, carabi

Refrain

Fellow Guilleri
(English Translation)

There was a little man
Who was called Guilleri, carabi,
He went a-hunting
A-hunting partridges, carabi.

(Chorus)
Titi, carabi, toto carabo*, fellow Guilleri
Will you let, will you let, will you let yourself die?

He went a-hunting
A-hunting partridges, carabi,
He climbed up a tree
To see his hounds run, carabi.

(Chorus)

He climbed up a tree
To see his hounds run, carabi,
Then the branch broke
And Guilleri fell down, carabi.

(Chorus)

Then the branch broke
And Guilleri fell down, carabi,
He broke his leg
And dislocated his arm, carabi.

(Chorus)

He broke his leg
And dislocated his arm, carabi,
The ladies from the hospital
Came because of the noise, carabi.

(Chorus)

The ladies from the hospital
Came because of the noise, carabi,
One brings plaster
Another brings shredded linen, carabi.

(Chorus)

One brings plaster
Another brings shredded linen, carabi,
They bandaged his leg
And set his arm, carabi.

(Chorus)

They bandaged his leg
And set his arm, carabi,
To thank these ladies
Guilleri kissed them, carabi.

(Chorus)

To thank these ladies
Guilleri kissed them, carabi,
Here's the moral,
Of this nice story, carabi.

(Chorus)

Here's the moral,
Of this nice story, carabi.
It proves that through women
Man is always healed, carabi.

(Chorus)

Notes

*These are meaningless words.
**The song has this as "mouri" and "couri", instead of "mourir" and "courir".
***The song has this as "tombit" and "embrassit" instead of "tomba" and "embrassa", to keep the rhyme.

For more about Compère Guilleri, go to:
http://www.mamalisa.com/?t=es&p=117.

There, you'll find sheet music, an MP3 tune and a MIDI melody.

Dans la forêt lointaine (In the Faraway Forest)

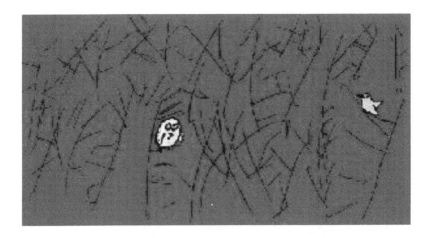

This is a canon for 3 voices. This song can be a canon for 4 voices if the two last lines are repeated.

Dans la forêt lointaine
(French Children's Song)

(1) Dans la forêt lointaine
On entend le coucou

(2) Du haut de son grand chêne
Il répond au hibou :

(3) "Coucou, coucou"
On entend le coucou.

In the Faraway Forest
(English Translation)

1. In the faraway forest
You can hear the cuckoo

2. From the top of the big oak
It answers the owl:

3. "Cuckoo, cuckoo"*
You can hear the cuckoo.

Notes

*In French "coucou" is the name of the bird and it's also the "song" that he sings. It can also mean "peek-a-boo" or "hi".

Comments

There's another version with the last 2 lines sung differently:

(1) Dans la forêt lointaine
On entend le coucou

(2) Du haut de son grand chêne
Il répond au hibou :

(3) "COUCOU HIBOU, COUCOU HIBOU,
COUCOU HIBOU, COUCOU."

English Translation:

1. In the faraway forest
You can hear the cuckoo

2. From the top of the big oak
It answers the owl:

3. "CUCKOO OWL, CUCKOO OWL,
CUCKOO OWL, CUCKOO."

The last two lines can either be understood as a call-and-answer, with the owl calling "cuckoo" and the cuckoo calling back "owl", or it can be understood as only the cuckoo calling, "Cuckoo owl, cuckoo owl". In the latter case, "cuckoo" can also mean "peek-a-boo" or "hi!".

For more about Dans la forêt lointaine, go to:
http://www.mamalisa.com/?t=es&p=627.

There, you'll find sheet music, an MP3 tune, a MIDI melody and a video performance.

Douce nuit (Sweet Night)

*Here's a well-known French version of the German Austrian song "**Stille Nacht** (http://www.mamalisa.com/?t=es&p=2751&c=38)" **(Silent Night in English)** (http://www.mamalisa.com/?t=es&p=1298&c=23). The original version was written as a poem by Joseph Mohr in 1816 and set to music by his friend Franz Gruber in 1818. The French lyrics are by Rev. Father Barjon.*

Douce nuit
(French Christmas Carol)

Douce nuit, sainte nuit !
Dans les cieux ! L'astre luit.
Le mystère annoncé s'accomplit
Cet enfant sur la paille endormi,
C'est l'amour infini !

C'est l'amour infini !

Saint enfant, doux agneau !
Qu'il est grand ! Qu'il est beau !
Entendez résonner les pipeaux
Des bergers conduisant leurs troupeaux
Vers son humble berceau !
Vers son humble berceau !

C'est vers nous qu'il accourt,
En un don sans retour !
De ce monde ignorant de l'amour,
Où commence aujourd'hui son séjour,
Qu'il soit Roi pour toujours !
Qu'il soit Roi pour toujours !

Quel accueil pour un Roi !
Point d'abri, point de toit !
Dans sa crèche, il grelotte de froid
Ô pécheur, sans attendre la croix,
Jésus souffre pour toi !
Jésus souffre pour toi !

Paix à tous ! Gloire au ciel !
Gloire au sein maternel,
Qui pour nous, en ce jour de Noël,
Enfanta le Sauveur éternel,
Qu'attendait Israël !
Qu'attendait Israël !

Sweet Night
(English Translation)

Sweet night, holy night!
In the heavens the star shines.
The announced rite has been fulfilled,
This child asleep on the straw
Is infinite love!
Is infinite love!

Holy child, sweet lamb!
How great! How beautiful!
Hear the sound of the reed-pipes,
Of the shepherds who lead their flocks
To his humble cradle!
To his humble cradle!

He comes to us
As an unrequited gift.
To this world that doesn't know love
Where today he begins his sojourn
Let him be King forever!

Let him be King forever!

What a welcome for a King!
No shelter, no roof!
In his crib he shivers from the cold,
O sinner, without waiting for the cross,
Jesus suffers for you!
Jesus suffers for you!

Peace onto all! Glory be to heaven!
Glory be to the Mother
Who, for us on this Christmas day,
Gave birth to the eternal Savior
That Israel was expecting!
That Israel was expecting!

For more about Douce nuit, go to: **http://www.mamalisa.com/?t=es&p=2967**.

There, you'll find sheet music, an MP3 tune, a MIDI melody and a video performance.

17

Frère Jacques (Brother John)

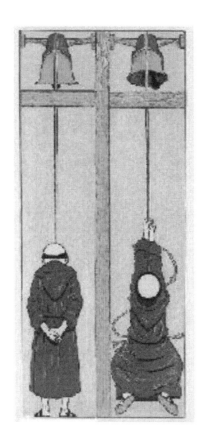

Frère Jacques
(French Children's Song)

Frère Jacques,
Frère Jacques,
Dormez-vous?
Dormez-vous?
Sonnez les matines.
Sonnez les matines.
Ding, ding, dong.
Ding, ding, dong.

Brother John

(English Translation)

Are you sleeping,
Are you sleeping,
Brother John?
Brother John?
Morning bells are ringing.
Morning bells are ringing.
Ding, dong, ding.
Ding, dong, ding.

Notes

The English "translation" above is actually the English version, not the literal translation. Here's the literal English translation of Frère Jacques:

Brother James,
Brother James,
Are you sleeping?
Are you sleeping?
Ring the morning bells,
Ring the morning bells,
Ding ding dong,
Ding ding dong.

Comments

*Here's a **recording of Frère Jacques sung in both French and English** (http://www.mamalisa.com/mp3/frere_jacques_areyousleeping_ezwa_lib.mp3) (by Ezwa).*

*The CLasse d'INitiation de Mons-en-Baroeul/Lille Fives in France has a Frère Jacques page that contains videos of students and teachers singing Frère Jacques in different languages. **Click here to visit the page** (http://demonsaumonde.free.fr/frere.jacques/index.html).*

For more about Frère Jacques, go to: **http://www.mamalisa.com/?t=es&p=180**.

There, you'll find sheet music and an MP3 tune.

Gentil coquelicot (Nice Poppy)

This song is also called J'AI DESCENDU DANS MON JARDIN *(I went down to my garden)...*

Gentil coquelicot
(French Children's Song)

J'ai descendu dans mon jardin
J'ai descendu dans mon jardin
Pour y cueillir du romarin.

Refrain
Gentil coqu'licot mesdames
Gentil coqu'licot nouveau
Gentil coqu'licot mesdames
Gentil coqu'licot nouveau.

Pour y cueillir du romarin
Pour y cueillir du romarin
J' n'en avais pas cueilli trois brins.

Refrain

J' n'en avais pas cueilli trois brins
J' n'en avais pas cueilli trois brins
Qu'un rossignol vint sur ma main.

Refrain

Qu'un rossignol vint sur ma main
Qu'un rossignol vint sur ma main
Il me dit trois mots en latin.

Refrain

Il me dit trois mots en latin
Il me dit trois mots en latin
Que les hommes ne valent rien.

Refrain

Que les hommes ne valent rien
Que les hommes ne valent rien
Et les garçons encore bien moins.

Refrain

Et les garçons encore bien moins
Et les garçons encore bien moins
Des dames il ne me dit rien.

Refrain

Des dames il ne me dit rien
Des dames il ne me dit rien
Mais des d'moiselles beaucoup de bien.

Nice Poppy
(English Translation)

I went down to my garden
I went down to my garden
To gather some rosemary.

(Chorus)
Nice poppy, ladies
Nice new poppy,
Nice poppy, ladies
Nice new poppy.

To gather some rosemary
To gather some rosemary,
I hadn't picked three sprigs.

(Chorus)

I hadn't picked three sprigs
I hadn't picked three sprigs
When a nightingale landed on my hand.

(Chorus)

When a nightingale landed on my hand
When a nightingale landed on my hand
It told me three words in Latin.

(Chorus)

It told me three words in Latin
It told me three words in Latin
That men are worthless.

(Chorus)

That men are worthless
That men are worthless
And boys are worth even less.

(Chorus)

And boys are worth even less
And boys are worth even less,
It told me nothing about ladies.

(Chorus)

It told me nothing about ladies
It told me nothing about ladies,
But a lot of good things about maidens.

(Chorus)

Photos & Illustrations

For more about Gentil coquelicot, go to:
http://www.mamalisa.com/?t=es&p=142.

There, you'll find sheet music, an MP3 tune and a MIDI melody.

Il court le furet (The Ferret Runs)

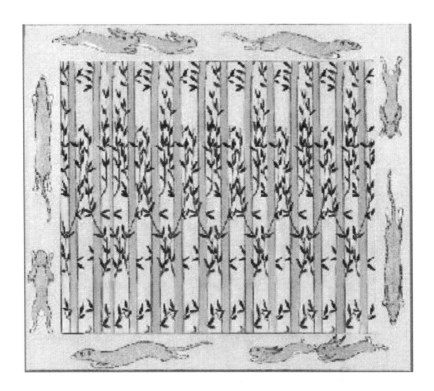

There are two versions of this song in the lyrics below.

Il court le furet
(French Children's Song)

Refrain:
Il court il court le furet
Le furet du bois, mesdames
Il court il court le furet
Le furet du bois joli

Il est passé par ici
Le furet du bois, mesdames
Il est passé par ici
Le furet du bois joli

Refrain:

Il court il court le furet
Le furet du bois, mesdames
Il court il court le furet
Le furet du bois joli

Il repassera par là
Le furet du bois, mesdames
Devinez s'il est ici
le furet du bois joli

Refrain:
Il court il court le furet
Le furet du bois, mesdames
Il court il court le furet
Le furet du bois joli

Le furet est bien caché
Le furet du bois, mesdames
Pourras-tu le retrouver?
Le furet du bois joli.

AUTRE VERSION

Il court il court le furet
Le furet du bois, mesdames
Il court il court le furet
Le furet du bois joli
Il est passé par ici
Il repassera par là.

The Ferret Runs
(English Translation)

(Chorus)
The ferret, it runs, it runs,
The ferret of the woods, my ladies,
The ferret, it runs, it runs,
The ferret of the pretty woods.

It passed by here
The ferret of the woods, my ladies,
It passed by here,
The ferret of the pretty woods.

(Chorus)
The ferret, it runs, it runs,
The ferret of the woods, my ladies,
The ferret, it runs, it runs,
The ferret of the pretty woods.

It'll pass again over there,
The ferret of the woods, my ladies,

Guess if it's here,
The ferret of the pretty woods.

(Chorus)
The ferret, it runs, it runs,
The ferret of the woods, my ladies,
The ferret, it runs, it runs,
The ferret of the pretty woods.

The ferret is well hidden,
The ferret of the woods, my ladies,
Will you be able to find it?
The ferret of the pretty woods.

ANOTHER VERSION:

The ferret, it runs, it runs,
The ferret of the woods, my ladies,
The ferret, it runs, it runs,
The ferret of the pretty woods.
It passed by here,
It'll pass again over there.

Game Instructions

First slip a ring on a long string and tie both ends. To determine the length of the string, you need to use about 20" of string (50cm) per player.

The children make a circle around one child in the center. The kids standing in the circle hold the string with both hands. So there will be one long circle of string that's held by the kids. The kids pass the ring along the string from hand to hand. The child in the middle has to guess who has the ring.

As soon as the child in the center guesses who has the ring, he says so and the two children switch spots.

For more about Il court le furet, go to: **http://www.mamalisa.com/?t=es&p=118**.

There, you'll find sheet music, an MP3 tune, a MIDI melody and a video performance.

Il était un petit navire (There Was a Little Ship)

In this song, the singer can choose when to sing the chorus. Some people sing it after each verse, some sing it after every 2 or 3 verses and some people don't sing it at all.

Il était un petit navire
(French Children's Song)

Il était un petit navire
Il était un petit navire
Qui n'avait ja-ja-jamais navigué
Qui n'avait ja-ja-jamais navigué.
Ohé ohé!

Refrain
Ohé ohé ohé ohé matelot
Matelot navigue sur les flots
Ohé ohé ohé ohé matelot
Matelot navigue sur les flots.

Il entreprit un long voyage
Il entreprit un long voyage
Sur la mer Mé-Mé-Méditerranée
Sur la mer Mé-Mé-Méditerranée.
Ohé ohé

Au bout de cinq à six semaines
Au bout de cinq à six semaines
Les vivres vin-vin-vinrent à manquer
Les vivres vin-vin-vinrent à manquer.

On tira-z-à la courte paille
On tira-z-à la courte paille
Pour savoir qui-qui-qui serait mangé
Pour savoir qui-qui-qui serait mangé.
Ohé ohé

Le sort tomba sur le plus jeune
Le sort tomba sur le plus jeune
Bien qu'il ne fût pas très épais
Bien qu'il ne fût pas très épais.

On cherche alors à quelle sauce
On cherche alors à quelle sauce
Le pauvre enfant-fant-fant serait mangé
Le pauvre enfant-fant-fant serait mangé.

L'un voulait qu'on le mît à frire
L'un voulait qu'on le mît à frire
L'autre voulait-lait-lait le fricasser
L'autre voulait-lait-lait le fricasser.
Ohé ohé

Pendant qu'ainsi on délibère
Pendant qu'ainsi on délibère
Il monta sur sur sur le grand hunier
Il monta sur sur sur le grand hunier.

Il fit au ciel une prière
Il fit au ciel une prière
Interrogeant-geant-geant l'immensité
Interrogeant-geant-geant l'immensité.

Ô sainte Vierge, ô ma patronne
Ô sainte Vierge, ô ma patronne
Empêchez-les les les de me manger
Empêchez-les les les de me manger.

Au même instant un grand miracle
Au même instant un grand miracle
Pour l'enfant fut fut fut réalisé
Pour l'enfant fut fut fut réalisé.

Des p'tits poissons dans le navire
Des p'tits poissons dans le navire
Sautèrent bien-bien-bientôt par milliers
Sautèrent bien-bien-bientôt par milliers.

On les prit, on les mit à frire

On les prit, on les mit à frire
Et le p'tit mou-mou-mousse fut sauvé
Et le p'tit mou-mou-mousse fut sauvé.

There Was a Little Ship
(English Translation)

There was a little ship,
There was a little ship
That had never sailed
That had never sailed.
Ahoy! Ahoy!

(Chorus)
Ahoy, ahoy, ahoy matey,
Matey sails the sea.
Ahoy, ahoy, ahoy matey,
Matey sails the sea.

It undertook a long voyage,
It undertook a long voyage
On the Mediterranean Sea,
On the Mediterranean Sea.
Ahoy! Ahoy!

After five or six weeks,
After five or six weeks
The food ran out,
The food ran out.

They drew straws,
They drew straws
To find out who would be eaten,
To find out who would be eaten.
Ahoy! Ahoy!

The short straw went to the youngest one,
The short straw went to the youngest one,
Although he wasn't very fat,
Although he wasn't very fat.

They tried to figure out with which sauce,
They tried to figure out with which sauce
The poor child should be cooked,
The poor child should be cooked.

One wanted him fried,
One wanted him fried,
The other wanted him fricasseed,
The other wanted him fricasseed.
Ahoy! Ahoy!

While they were deliberating,
While they were deliberating,
He climbed to the topsail,
He climbed to the topsail.

He prayed to the heavens,
He prayed to the heavens
Pleading with the vastness
Pleading with the vastness.

O Holy Virgin, O, My Lady,
O Holy Virgin, O, My Lady,
Keep them from eating me,
Keep them from eating me.

At that moment, a great miracle,
At that moment, a great miracle
Was performed for the child
Was performed for the child.

Soon, little fish jumped,
Soon, little fish jumped
Into the ship by the thousands,
Into the ship by the thousands.

They were gathered, they were fried,
They were gathered, they were fried
And the ship's young boy was saved,
And the ship's young boy was saved.

For more about Il était un petit navire, go to:
http://www.mamalisa.com/?t=es&p=139.

There, you'll find sheet music, an MP3 tune, a MIDI melody and a video performance.

Il était une bergère (There Was a Shepherdess)

Il était une bergère
(French Children's Song)

Il était une bergère,
Et ron, ron, ron, petit patapon.
Il était une bergère,
Qui gardait ses moutons,
Ron, Ron,
Qui gardait ses moutons.

Elle fit un fromage,
Et ron, ron, ron, petit patapon.
Elle fit un fromage,
Du lait de ses moutons,
Ron, Ron,
Du lait de ses moutons.

Le chat qui la regarde,
Et ron, ron, ron, petit patapon.
Le chat qui la regarde,

D'un petit air fripon,
Ron, Ron,
D'un petit air fripon.

Si tu y mets la patte,
Et ron, ron, ron, petit patapon.
Si tu y mets la patte,
Tu auras du bâton,
Ron, Ron,
Tu auras du bâton.

Il n'y mit pas la patte,
Et ron, ron, ron, petit patapon.
Il n'y mit pas la patte,
Il y mis le menton,
Ron, Ron,
Il y mis le menton.

La bergère en colère,
Et ron, ron, ron, petit patapon.
La bergère en colère,
Tua son p'tit chaton,
Ron, Ron,
Tua son p'tit chaton.

Elle fut à confesse,
Et ron, ron, ron, petit patapon.
Elle fut à confesse,
Pour demander pardon,
Ron, Ron,
Pour demander pardon.

- Mon Père, je m'accuse,
Et ron, ron, ron, petit patapon.
Mon Père, je m'accuse,
D'avoir tué mon chaton,
Ron, Ron,
D'avoir tué mon chaton.

- Ma fille, pour pénitence,
Et ron, ron, ron, petit patapon.
Ma fille, pour pénitence,
Nous nous embrasserons,
Ron, Ron,
Nous nous embrasserons.

- La pénitence est douce,
Et ron, ron, ron, petit patapon.
La pénitence est douce,
Nous recommencerons,
Ron, Ron,
Nous recommencerons.

There Was a Shepherdess
(English Translation)

There was a shepherdess,
And ron, ron, ron, little patapon.
There was a shepherdess,
Who was watching her sheep,
Ron, ron,
Who was watching her sheep.

She made cheese,
And ron, ron, ron, little patapon.
She made cheese
With her sheep's milk
Ron, ron,
With her sheep's milk.

The cat was watching her,
And ron, ron, ron, little patapon.
The cat was watching her
With a mischievous look
Ron, ron,
With a mischievous look.

"If you put your paw in it
And ron, ron, ron, little patapon.
If you put your paw in it,
I'll beat you with a stick
Ron, ron,
I'll beat you with a stick."

It didn't put its paw in it,
And ron, ron, ron, little patapon.
It didn't put its paw in it,
It put its chin in it,
Ron, ron,
It put its chin in it.

The angry shepherdess,
And ron, ron, ron, little patapon.
The angry shepherdess
Killed her little kitten,
Ron, ron,
Killed her little kitten.

She went to confession,
And ron, ron, ron, little patapon.
She went to confession
To ask for a pardon,
Ron, ron,
To ask for a pardon.

"Father, I accuse myself,

And ron, ron, ron, little patapon.
Father, I accuse myself
Of killing my kitten,
Ron, ron,
Of killing my kitten."

"Daughter, as a penance,
And ron, ron, ron, little patapon.
Daughter, as a penance
We'll kiss each other,
Ron, ron,
We'll kiss each other."

"The penance is sweet,
And ron, ron, ron, little patapon.
The penance is sweet,
We'll do it over again,
Ron, ron,
We'll do it over again."

Notes

Not very moral, is it?

*****

Alternate Ending:

Harald Meilicke wrote: "'Il était une bergère' has a text that was unknown to me and is a slightly, let's say, mean version starting from 'la bergère en colère tua son p'tit chaton' onwards (i.e., she kills the kitten and later says she'll do it again). In a version more appropriate for small children, this couplet goes 'la bergère en colère lui donna du bâton' (i.e. she beats the kitten) and the songs ends."

Comments

There's an English Version of IL ÉTAIT UNE BERGÈRE *called* **There Was a Farmer's Daughter** *(http://www.mamalisa.com/blog/there-was-a-farmers-daughter-il-tait-une-bergre/). (Check out the link!)*

There's a Spanish song with the same theme called **Estaba una pastora** *(http://mamalisa.com/?t=es&p=2523&c=71).*

For more about Il était une bergère, go to:
http://www.mamalisa.com/?t=es&p=2524.

There, you'll find sheet music, an MP3 tune and a MIDI melody.

Il était un' dame Tartine (There Was a Lady Slice of Bread)

This song is from the 1st half of the 19th century...

Il était un' dame Tartine
(French Children's Song)

Il était un' dame Tartine
Dans un beau palais de beurr' frais
La muraille était de praline,
Le parquet était de croquets,
La chambre à coucher
De crème de lait,
Le lit de biscuits,
Les rideaux d'anis.

Quand elle s'en allait à la ville
Elle avait un petit bonnet
Les rubans étaient de pastilles
Et le fond de bon raisiné;
Sa petit' carriole
Était d' croquignoles,

Ses petits chevaux
Étaient d' pâtés chauds

Elle épousa monsieur Gimblette
Coiffé d'un beau fromage blanc
Son chapeau était de galette
Son habit était d' vol-au-vent
Culotte en nougat
Gilet d' chocolat,
Bas de caramel
Et souliers de miel.

Leur fille, la belle Charlotte
Avait un nez de massepain,
De très belles dents de compote,
Des oreilles de craquelin
Je la vois garnir
Sa rob' de plaisirs
Avec un rouleau
De pâte d'abricots.

Le puissant prince Limonade
Bien frisé, vient lui faire sa cour
Ses longs cheveux de marmelade
Ornés de pomm' cuites au four
Son royal bandeau
De petits gâteaux
Et de raisins secs
Portait au respect.

On frémit en voyant sa garde
De câpres et de cornichons
Armés de fusils de moutarde
Et de sabr's en pelur's d'oignons
Sur de bell's brioches
Charlott' vient s'asseoir ,
Les bonbons d' ses poches
Sortent jusqu'au soir.

Voici que la fée Carabosse
Jalouse et de mauvaise humeur
Renversa d'un coup de sa bosse
Le palais sucré du bonheur
Pour le rebâtir
Donnez à loisir,
Donnez, bons parents
Du sucre aux enfants !

There Was a Lady Slice of Bread
(English Translation)

There was a Lady Slice of Bread
In a beautiful palace of fresh butter,
The wall was made of praline
The floor was made of biscotti,
The bedroom was made out of
The cream-top of milk,
The bed was made of cookies
The curtains, anise candy.

When she went to the city
She wore a little cap,
The ribbons were made of suckers
And the base was grape preserves,
Her little cart
Was hard crunchy cookies
Her little horses
Were made of pâté pies.

She married Mister Ring-cookie
His hair was beautiful cottage cheese,
His hat was a flat French cake,
His suit was made of canapés:
Pants of nougat,
Vest of chocolate,
Stockings of caramel
And shoes of honey.

Their daughter, the beautiful Charlotte
Had a nose of marzipan,
Very beautiful teeth of compote,
Ears of crackers,
I see her garnish
Her leisure dress
With a roll
Of apricot paste.

The mighty, curly-haired prince Lemonade
Comes to court her,
He has long hair of marmalade,
Decorated with baked apples.
His royal headband,
Made of cupcakes
And raisins,
Brings respect.

One shudders seeing his Guard
Made of capers and gherkins
Armed with mustard rifles
And onion peel sabres.
On nice buns,
Charlotte came to sit down.
The candy in her pockets
Came tumbling out till nighttime.

All of a sudden the Wicked Fairy,
Jealous and bad-tempered,
Used her hump to knock over
The sweet palace of happiness.
To rebuild it:
Give at leisure,
Give, good parents,
Sugar to the children!

Notes

Check out MAMA LISA'S WORLD BLOG *to see* ***photos and descriptions of the foods in Il était un' dame Tartine*** *(http://www.mamalisa.com/blog/english-equivalents-to-french-pastries-sweets/).*

Comments

This song reminds me of the Scottish song called ***Aiken Drum*** *(http://www.mamalisa.com/?t=es&p=777&c=110) where the man is also made out of food! -Mama Lisa*

For more about Il était un' dame Tartine, go to:
http://www.mamalisa.com/?t=es&p=3073.

There, you'll find sheet music, an MP3 tune, a MIDI melody and a video performance.

J'ai du bon tabac (I Have Good Tobacco)

The tobacco in this song is in the form of snuff.

J'ai du bon tabac
(French Children's Song)

J'ai du bon tabac dans ma tabatière
J'ai du bon tabac, tu n'en auras pas

J'en ai du fin et du bien râpé
Mais ce n'est pas pour ton vilain nez

J'ai du bon tabac dans ma tabatière
J'ai du bon tabac, tu n'en auras pas

I Have Good Tobacco
(English Translation)

I have good tobacco in my snuff box,
I have good tobacco and you will get none.

I have some fine, and some well-shredded,
But they are not for your ugly nose.

I have good tobacco in my snuff box,
I have good tobacco and you will get none.

Notes

The lyrics to this song are attributed to Gabriel Charles, the Abbot of L'Attaignant (1697-1779). Anonymous music from the 17th century.

For more about J'ai du bon tabac, go to:
http://www.mamalisa.com/?t=es&p=3100.

There, you'll find sheet music, an MP3 tune and a MIDI melody.

J'ai perdu le do de ma clarinette (I Lost the C on My Clarinet)

There are two versions of this song both of which you can find below...

J'ai perdu le do de ma clarinette
(French Children's Marching Song)

J'ai perdu le do de ma clarinette,
J'ai perdu le do de ma clarinette,
Ah ! si papa il savait ça, tralala,
Ah ! si papa il savait ça, tralala,
Il dirait: Ohé !
Il dirait: Ohé !
Tu n' connais pas la cadence,
Tu n' sais pas comment l'on danse,
Tu n' sais pas danser
Au pas cadencé !
Au pas, camarade, au pas, camarade,
Au pas, au pas, au pas
Au pas, camarade, au pas, camarade,
Au pas, au pas, au pas, au pas, au pas.

J'ai perdu le ré de ma clarinette,
J'ai perdu le ré de ma clarinette,
Ah ! si papa il savait ça, tralala,
Ah ! si papa il savait ça, tralala,
Il dirait: Ohé !
Il dirait: Ohé !
Tu n' connais pas la cadence,
Tu n'sais pas comment l'on danse,
Tu n'sais pas danser
Au pas cadencé !
Au pas, camarade, au pas, camarade,
Au pas, au pas, au pas
Au pas, camarade, au pas, camarade,
Au pas, au pas, au pas, au pas, au pas.

J'ai perdu le mi de ma clarinette…

J'ai perdu le fa de ma clarinette…

J'ai perdu le sol de ma clarinette…

J'ai perdu le la de ma clarinette…

J'ai perdu le si de ma clarinette…

I Lost the C on My Clarinet
(English Translation)

I lost the C on my clarinet,
I lost the C on my clarinet,
Oh! If Daddy knew about that, tra la la,
Oh! If Daddy knew about that, tra la la,
He would say, "Oh, hey!"
He would say, "Oh, hey!"
You don't know the tempo,
You don't know how to dance,
You really can't dance
In slow time!
March, comrade, march, comrade,
March, march, march.
March, comrade, march, comrade,
March, march, march, march, march.

I lost the D on my clarinet,
I lost the D on my clarinet,
Oh! If Daddy knew about that, tra la la,
Oh! If Daddy knew about that, tra la la!
He would say, "Oh, hey!"
He would say, "Oh, hey!"
You don't know the tempo,
You don't know how to dance,
You really can't dance
In slow time!
March, comrade, march, comrade,
March, march, march.
March, comrade, march, comrade,
March, march, march, march, march.

I lost the E on my clarinet…

I lost the F on my clarinet…

I lost the G on my clarinet…

I lost the A on my clarinet…

I lost the B on my clarinet...

Notes

2nd Version:

J'ai perdu le do de ma clarinette,
J'ai perdu le do de ma clarinette,
Ah ! si papa il savait ça, tralala,
Ah ! si papa il savait ça, tralala,
Il dirait: Ohé !
Il dirait: Ohé !
Au pas, camarade, au pas, camarade,
Au pas, au pas, au pas
Au pas, camarade, au pas, camarade,
Au pas, au pas, au pas, au pas, au pas.

English Translation:

I lost the C on my clarinet,
I lost the C on my clarinet,
Oh! If Daddy knew about that, tra la la,
Oh! If Daddy knew about that, tra la la,
He would say, "Oh, hey!"
He would say, "Oh, hey!"
March, comrade, march, comrade,
March, march, march.
March, comrade, march, comrade,
March, march, march, march, march.

Photos & Illustrations

For more about J'ai perdu le do de ma clarinette, go to:
http://www.mamalisa.com/?t=es&p=2521.

There, you'll find sheet music, an MP3 tune and a MIDI melody.

J'ai vu le loup, le renard, le lièvre (I Saw the Wolf, The Fox, The Hare)

Some sources believe the wolf, the fox and the hare in this song represented the King, the Lord and the Church. In the old days, these were all authorities who collected taxes, leaving nothing for the peasants.

J'ai vu le loup, le renard, le lièvre
(French Children's Song)

J'ai vu le loup, le renard, le lièvre,
J'ai vu le loup, le renard cheuler*.
C'est moi-même qui les ai rebeuillés*.
J'ai vu le loup, le renard, le lièvre,
C'est moi-même qui les ai rebeuillés.
J'ai vu le loup, le renard cheuler.

J'ai ouï* le loup, le renard, le lièvre,
J'ai ouï le loup, le renard chanter.
C'est moi-même qui les ai rechignés,*
J'ai ouï le loup, le renard, le lièvre,
C'est moi-même qui les ai rechignés,
J'ai ouï le loup, le renard chanter.

J'ai vu le loup, le renard, le lièvre,
J'ai vu le loup, le renard danser,
C'est moi-même qui les ai revirés,*
J'ai vu le loup, le renard, le lièvre,

C'est moi-même qui les ai revirés,
J'ai vu le loup, le renard danser.

I Saw the Wolf, The Fox, The Hare
(English Translation)

I saw the wolf, the fox, the hare
I saw the wolf, the fox drinking
I spied on them myself.
I saw the wolf, the fox, the hare,
I spied on them myself,
I saw the wolf, the fox drinking.

I heard the wolf, the fox, the hare,
I heard the wolf, the fox singing
I imitated them myself.
I heard the wolf, the fox, the hare,
I imitated them myself,
I heard the wolf, the fox singing.

I saw the wolf, the fox, the hare,
I saw the wolf, the fox dancing
I made them dance myself.
I saw the wolf, the fox, the hare,
I made them dance myself,
I saw the wolf, the fox dancing.

Notes

*The words marked with asterisks are old verbs no longer in use.

Sometimes the hare is a weasel in this song, as in the version below...

J'ai vu le loup, le renard et la belette,
J'ai vu le loup et le renard danser.
J'ai vu le loup, le renard et la belette,
J'ai vu le loup et le renard danser.
J' les ai vus taper du pied,
J'ai vu le loup, le renard et la belette,
J'ai vu le loup et le renard danser.

SINGABLE TRANSLATION

I saw the wolf, and the fox and the weasel,
I saw the wolf and the fox dancing.
I saw the wolf, and the fox and the weasel,
I saw the wolf and the fox dancing.
I saw them stamping their feet,
I saw the wolf, and the fox and the weasel,
I saw the wolf and the fox dancing.

******

*There's an **Occitan version of J'ai vu le loup, le renard, le lièvre** here (http://mamalisa.com/?t=es&p=2170&c=72).*

Comments

There are even more versions of this song!

For more about J'ai vu le loup, le renard, le lièvre, go to:
http://www.mamalisa.com/?t=es&p=2171.

There, you'll find sheet music, an MP3 tune and a MIDI melody.

J'aime la galette (I Love Cake)

Since the Middle Ages, in celebration of the Epiphany (aka Kings' Day), French people have eaten GALETTES DES ROIS (Kings' Cake). Here is a song called J'AIME LA GALETTE (I Love Cake) that French kids sing on Kings' Day!

J'aime la galette
(French Kings' Day Song)

J'aime la galette,
Savez-vous comment ?
Quand elle est bien faite
Avec du beurre dedans.
Trala la la la la la la lère,
Tra la la la la la la la la,
Tra la la la la la la la lère,
Tra la la la la la la la la.

I Love Cake
(English Translation)

I love cake,
Do you know how?

When it's made well,
With butter inside!
Tra la la la la la la lère,
Tra la la la la la la la,
Tra la la la la la la lère,
Tra la la la la la la la.

Notes

*You can find Mama Lisa's **Recipe for Kings Cake (Galette des Rois)** (http://www.mamalisa.com/blog/kings-day-in-france-and-a-recipe-for-french-kings-cake/) on our blog.*

For more about J'aime la galette, go to:
http://www.mamalisa.com/?t=es&p=782.

There, you'll find sheet music, an MP3 tune, a MIDI melody and a video performance.

Jean Petit qui danse (John Petit)

Jean Petit (in English, John Little) was the name of a real man who lived in the 17th century. But since "petit" means "short or little", some French people think of "Jean Petit" as "Little John" instead of "John Little".

Jean Petit qui danse
(French Children's Song)

Jean Petit qui danse
Jean Petit qui danse
De son doigt il danse
De son doigt il danse
De son doigt, doigt, doigt,
De son doigt, doigt, doigt,

De son doigt, doigt, doigt,
Ainsi danse Jean Petit

Jean Petit qui danse
Jean Petit qui danse
De sa main il danse
De sa main il danse
De sa main, main, main,
De son doigt, doigt, doigt,
De son doigt, doigt, doigt,
De son doigt, doigt, doigt,
Ainsi danse Jean Petit.

Jean Petit qui danse
Jean Petit qui danse
De son bras il danse
De son bras il danse
De son bras, bras, bras,
De sa main, main, main,
De son doigt, doigt, doigt,
De son doigt, doigt, doigt,
De son doigt, doigt, doigt,
Ainsi danse Jean Petit.

ET AINSI DE SUITE AVEC SON PIED, SA JAMBE ET TOUTES LES PARTIES DU CORPS QU'ON VEUT BIEN AJOUTER

John Petit
(English Translation)

John Petit is dancing
John Petit is dancing,
With his finger he is dancing,
With his finger he is dancing,
With his finger, finger, finger,
With his finger, finger, finger,
With his finger, finger, finger,
John Petit dances this way.

John Petit is dancing
John Petit is dancing,
With his hand he is dancing,
With his hand he is dancing,
With his hand, hand, hand,
With his finger, finger, finger,
With his finger, finger, finger,
With his finger, finger, finger,
John Petit dances this way.

John Petit is dancing
John Petit is dancing,
With his arm he's dancing,

With his arm he's dancing,
With his arm, arm, arm,
With his hand, hand, hand,
With his finger, finger, finger,
With his finger, finger, finger,
With his finger, finger, finger,
John Petit dances this way.

AND SO ON WITH HIS FOOT, LEG, AND ANY OTHER BODY PART THAT YOU WANT TO ADD.

Notes

Another Version:

Jean Petit qui danse
Jean Petit qui danse
Pour le roi de France
Pour le roi de France
De son pied, pied, pied
De son doigt, doigt, doigt
Ainsi danse Jean Petit.

Jean Petit qui danse
Jean Petit qui danse,
Pour le roi de France
Pour le roi de France,
De sa jambe, jambe, jambe
De son pied, pied, pied
De son doigt, doigt, doigt
Ainsi danse Jean Petit.

Jean Petit qui danse
Jean Petit qui danse,
Pour le roi de France
Pour le roi de France,
De sa cuisse, cuisse, cuisse
De sa jambe, jambe, jambe
De son pied, pied, pied
De son doigt, doigt, doigt
Ainsi danse Jean Petit…

ET AINSI DE SUITE AVEC SON VENTRE, SA MAIN ET TOUTES LES PARTIES DU CORPS QU'ON VEUT BIEN AJOUTER.

English Translation:

John Petit is dancing
John Petit is dancing,
For the king of France
For the king of France,
With his foot, foot, foot,

With his finger, finger, finger,
John Petit dances this way.

John Petit is dancing
John Petit is dancing,
For the king of France
For the king of France,
With his foot, foot, foot,
With his leg, leg, leg,
With his finger, finger, finger,
John Petit dances this way.

John Petit is dancing
John Petit is dancing,
For the king of France
For the king of France,
With his foot, foot, foot,
With his leg, leg, leg,
With his thigh, thigh, thigh,
With his finger, finger, finger,
John Petit dances this way.

AND SO ON WITH HIS BELLY, HIS HAND, AND ALL THE BODY PARTS YOU WANT TO ADD.

Game Instructions

The beginning of this song is sung while dancing around in a circle. Then when singing "de son doigt, doigt, doigt", the children touch the ground with their finger on each "doigt". Then when they sing the last "de son doigt, doigt, doigt", they point their finger to the sky. Next they turn around on "ainsi danse Jean Petit".

Each part of the body is used when its sung. Any part of the body can be added to make the children aware of their body parts.

Comments

"Jean Petit was a peasant in France. In 1643 in Villefranche de Rouergue, he led a peasant rebellion against King Louis XIV. When he lost and was taken prisoner, he was sentenced to torture by the wheel. The song says that when his finger was broken, he danced with his finger, etc." -Monique Palomares

For more about Jean Petit qui danse, go to:
http://www.mamalisa.com/?t=es&p=1798.

There, you'll find sheet music, an MP3 tune and a MIDI melody.

La bonne aventure ô gué (A Fine Adventure, Oh Joy!)

La bonne aventure ô gué
(French Children's Song)

Je suis un petit poupon
De bonne figure
Qui aime bien les bonbons
Et les confitures.
Si vous voulez m'en donner,
Je saurai bien les manger
La bonne aventure ô gué,
La bonne aventure.

Lorsque les petits garçons
Sont gentils et sages,
On leur donne des bonbons,
De belles images,
Mais quand il se font gronder
C'est le fouet qu'il faut donner.
La triste aventure ô gué,
La triste aventure.

Je serai sage et bien bon
Pour plaire à ma mère,
Je saurai bien ma leçon
Pour plaire à mon père.
Je veux bien les contenter
Et s'ils veulent m'embrasser,
La bonne aventure ô gué,
La bonne aventure.

A Fine Adventure, Oh Joy!
(English Translation)

I'm a little baby boy*
With a nice face,
Who likes candy
And jam.
If you want to give me some,
I'll know how to eat them.
A fine adventure, oh joy!**
A fine adventure.

When little boys
Are nice and smart,

They are given candy
And pretty pictures,
But when they are scolded
They must get the whip,
A sad adventure, oh joy,
A sad adventure.

I'll be smart and very good
To please my mother,
I'll learn my lessons well
To please my father.
I want to make them happy
And if they want to kiss me,
A fine adventure, oh joy!
A fine adventure.

Notes

Literally a little boy doll.
** "ô gué" is an old French expression that expresses joy and cheerfulness. (It can also be spelled "au gai" or "au gay".) It's traced back to the early 1500's. Nowadays, it's only found in the choruses of popular old songs.

For more about La bonne aventure ô gué, go to:
http://www.mamalisa.com/?t=es&p=2273.

There, you'll find sheet music, an MP3 tune and a MIDI melody.

La légende de Saint Nicolas (The Legend of Saint Nicholas)

La légende de Saint Nicolas
(French Children's Song)

Refrain:
Ils étaient trois petits enfants
Qui s'en allaient glaner aux champs.

1. Tant sont allés tant sont venus,
Que sur le soir se sont perdus.
S'en sont allés chez le boucher:
"Boucher voudrais-tu nous loger ?"

Refrain

2. "Entrez, entrez, petits enfants
Il y a d' la place assurément."
Ils n'étaient pas sitôt entrés,
Que le boucher les a tués.
AUTRE VERSION
Ils n'étaient pas sitôt entrés
Que le boucher les a tués
Les a coupés en p'tits morceaux,
Mis au saloir comme pourceaux

Refrain

3. Saint Nicolas au bout d' sept ans
Vint à passer dedans ce champ,
Alla frapper chez le boucher:
"Boucher voudrais-tu me loger ?"

Refrain

4. Entrez, entrez, Saint Nicolas,
Il y a d' la place, il n'en manqu' pas."
Il n'était pas sitôt entré
Qu'il a demandé à souper.

Refrain

5. "Du p'tit salé je veux avoir,
Qu'il y a sept ans qu'est au saloir".
Quand le boucher entendit ça,
Hors de sa porte il s'enfuya*

Refrain

6."Boucher, boucher, ne t'enfuis pas !
Repens-toi, Dieu te pardonnera".
Saint Nicolas alla s'asseoir
Dessus le bord de ce saloir

Refrain:

7."Petits enfants qui dormez là,
Je suis le grand Saint Nicolas."
Le grand saint étendit trois doigts,
Les p'tits se levèrent tous les trois.

Refrain

8. Le premier dit: "J'ai bien dormi".
Le second dit:" Et moi aussi".
A ajouté le plus petit:
"Je me croyais au paradis !"

Refrain

The Legend of Saint Nicholas
(English Translation)

(Chorus)
There were three little children
Who went a-gathering in the fields.

1. They went so much to, and so much fro,
That by the evening they had gotten lost.
They went to the butcher's house.
"Butcher, would you give us lodging?"

(Chorus)

2. "Come in, come in, little children
There's room, for sure."
No sooner had they come in,
Then the butcher killed them.
OTHER VERSION
No sooner had they come in,
Then the butcher killed them.
He cut them into small pieces,
Put them in the salting-tub as piglets.

(Chorus)

3. After seven years passed, Saint Nicholas
Happened to cross that field.
He went to knock on the butcher's door,
"Butcher, would you give me lodging?"

(Chorus)

4. "Come in, come in, Saint Nicholas.
There's room, no shortage of it."
No sooner had he come in,
Then he requested supper.

(Chorus)

5. "I want some of the salted meat
That's been in the salting-tub for seven years."
When the butcher heard that
He ran away from his house.

(Chorus)

6. "Butcher, butcher, don't run away!
Repent, God will forgive you."
Saint Nicholas went to sit down
On the edge of the salting-tub.

(Chorus)

7. "Little children who are sleeping here
I am the great Saint Nicholas."
The great saint stretched out three fingers.
The little ones got up, all three of them.

(Chorus)

8. The first one said "I slept well."
The second one said "And I did too."
The youngest one added:
"I thought I was in paradise!"

(Chorus)

Notes

It's "s'enfuya" instead of "s'enfuit" to keep the rhyme.

Comments

There's another version of this song you can read online (http://www.stnicholascenter.org/Brix?pageID=635).

For more about La légende de Saint Nicolas, go to:
http://www.mamalisa.com/?t=es&p=119.

There, you'll find sheet music and a MIDI melody.

La mère Michel (Old Ma Michel)

La mère Michel
(French Children's Song)

C'est la mèr' Michel qui a perdu son chat
Qui crie par la fenêtre qui le lui rendra

C'est le pèr' Lustucru qui lui a répondu :
"Allez, la mèr' Michel vot' chat n'est pas perdu."
Sur l'air du tra la la la
Sur l'air du tra la la la
Sur l'air du tradé-ri-dé-ra tra-la-la !

C'est la mèr' Michel qui lui a demandé :
"Mon chat n'est pas perdu vous l'avez donc trouvé ?"
C'est le pèr' Lustucru qui lui a répondu :
"Donnez un' récompense il vous sera rendu."
Sur l'air du tra la la la
Sur l'air du tra la la la
Sur l'air du trade-ri-dé-ra tra-la-la !

Alors la mèr' Michel lui dit : "C'est décidé,
Si vous rendez mon chat vous aurez un baiser."
Mais le pèr' Lustucru qui n'en a pas voulu
Lui dit : "Pour un lapin votre chat s'ra vendu!"
Sur l'air du tra la la la
Sur l'air du tra la la la
Sur l'air du trade-ri-dé-ra tra-la-la !

Old Ma Michel
(English Translation)

It's old ma Michel who lost her cat,
Who's yelling out the window, who will bring it back?
It's old man Lustucru who answered her:
"Come on, old ma Michel, your cat is not lost."
To the tune of tra la la la,
To the tune of tra la la la,
To the tune of tra-day-ree day-ra tra la la.

It's old ma Michel who asked him:
"My cat's not lost, you found it then?"
It's Old man Lustucru who answered her:
"Give a reward, it'll be returned to you."
To the tune of tra la la la,
To the tune of tra la la la,
To the tune of tra-day-ree day-ra tra la la.

Then old ma Michel told him: "It's settled
If you give my cat back, you'll get a kiss."
But old man Lustucru who didn't want one
Said to her: "Your cat will be sold as a rabbit!"
To the tune of tra la la la,
To the tune of tra la la la,
To the tune of tra-day-ree day-ra tra la la.

Notes

Monique wrote: "In the last verse in the 4th line, some versions go: "Lui dit 'La mère Michel, votre chat est vendu'" ("He said to her 'Old Ma Michel, your cat has been sold'").

Also, 'Lustucru' is the phonetic way to spell 'L'eusses-tu cru' ('Would you have believed it?'), meaning that this guy would do things that people wouldn't suspect he would do."

For more about La mère Michel, go to:
http://www.mamalisa.com/?t=es&p=160.

There, you'll find sheet music, an MP3 tune, a MIDI melody and a video performance.

Le bon roi Dagobert (The Good King Dagobert)

Le bon roi Dagobert
(French Children's Song)

Le bon roi Dagobert
Avait sa culotte à l'envers
Le grand saint Eloi lui dit :
"O mon roi, votre majesté
Est mal culottée"
"C'est vrai, lui dit le roi,
Je vais la remettre à l'endroit."

Le bon roi Dagobert
Chassait dans la plaine d'Anvers
Le grand saint Eloi lui dit :

"O mon roi, votre majesté
Est bien essoufflée"
"C'est vrai, lui dit le roi,
Un lapin courait après moi."

Le bon roi Dagobert
Voulait s'embarquer sur la mer
Le grand saint Eloi lui dit :
"O mon roi Votre majesté
Se fera noyer"
"C'est vrai, lui dit le roi,
On pourra crier : le roi boit !"

Le bon roi Dagobert
Mangeait en glouton du dessert
Le grand saint Eloi lui dit :
"O mon roi vous êtes gourmand
Ne mangez pas tant"
"C'est vrai, lui dit le roi,
Je ne le suis pas tant que toi"

Le bon roi Dagobert
Faisait des vers tout de travers
Le grand saint Eloi lui dit :
"O mon roi, laissez aux oisons
Faire des chansons"
"C'est vrai lui dit le roi,
C'est toi qui les feras pour moi."

Le bon roi Dagobert
Avait un grand sabre de fer
Le grand saint Eloi lui dit :
"O mon roi, votre majesté
Pourrait se blesser"
"C'est vrai lui dit le roi,
Qu'on me donne un sabre de bois."

Le bon roi Dagobert
Se battait à tort à travers
Le grand saint Eloi lui dit
"O mon roi, votre majesté
Se fera tuer"
"C'est vrai, lui dit le roi
Viens vite te mettre devant moi"

Le bon roi Dagobert
Craignait fort d'aller en enfer
Le grand saint Eloi lui dit :
"O mon roi, je crois bien, ma foi
Qu' vous irez tout droit"
"C'est vrai lui dit le roi,
Ne peux-tu pas prier pour moi ?"

Quand Dagobert mourut

Le diable aussitôt accourut
Le grand saint Eloi lui dit :
"O mon roi, Satan va passer
Faut vous confesser"
"Hélas, lui dit le roi,
Ne pourrais-tu mourir pour moi ?"

The Good King Dagobert
(English Translation)

The good King Dagobert
Had his breeches inside out.
The great Saint Eloy told him,
"Oh my king, your Majesty
Has his breeches inside out."
"Indeed," the king told him,
"I'm going to put them right side out."

The good King Dagobert
Was hunting in the Antwerp plain.
The great Saint Eloy told him,
"Oh my king, your Majesty
Is out of breath."
"Indeed," the king told him,
"A rabbit was running after me."

The good King Dagobert
Wanted to sail on the sea.
The great Saint Eloy told him,
"Oh my king, your Majesty
Will drown."
"Indeed," the king told him,
"They might yell, 'The king drinks!'"

The good King Dagobert
Was greedily eating his dessert.
The great Saint Eloy told him,
"Oh my king, you're greedy,
Don't eat so much."
"Indeed," the king told him,
"I'm not as greedy as you are."

The good King Dagobert
Was writing verses the wrong way.
The great Saint Eloy told him,
"Oh my king, let fools
Write songs."
"Indeed," the king told him,
"You will write them for me."

The good King Dagobert
Had a big iron saber.

The great Saint Eloy told him,
"Oh my king, your Majesty
Could get hurt."
"Indeed," the king told him,
"Let them give me a wooden saber."

The good King Dagobert
Was fighting wildly.
The great Saint Eloy told him,
"Oh my king, your Majesty
Will get killed."
"Indeed," the king told him,
"Come quickly and stand before me."

The good King Dagobert
Greatly feared going to hell.
The great Saint Eloy told him,
"Oh my king, I believe, by my faith,
That you'll go right there."
"Indeed," the king told him,
"Can't you pray for me?"

As soon as Dagobert died
The devil came running.
The great Saint Eloy told him,
"Oh my king, Satan's coming soon,
You have to confess."
"Alas," the king told him,
"Couldn't you die for me?"

Notes

Good King Dagobert was Dagobert the First, King of the Franks in the early 600's. Saint Eloi was Saint Eloy (aka St. Eligius). He was the Bishop of Noyon and chief councellor to King Dagobert. The song itself seems to go back to the French Revolution and is not about the actual King Dagobert.

For more about Le bon roi Dagobert, go to:
http://www.mamalisa.com/?t=es&p=2977.

There, you'll find sheet music, a MIDI melody and a video performance.

Le carillon de Vendôme (The Chimes of Vendôme)

This song takes place during The Hundred Years' War. It's about how Charles VII, the Dauphin prince, inherited the kingdom of France upon his father's death in 1422. At that point, the kingdom had been mainly reduced to the towns of Vendôme, Bourges, Orléans, Cléry and Beaugency. The rest of the kingdom was occupied by England and its allies.

This song dates back to the 15th or 16th century. It's sung to the tune of the church bells at the Trinity Church in Vendôme, France.

Le carillon de Vendôme
(French Round)

Mes amis que reste-t-il
À ce Dauphin si gentil ?
Orléans, Beaugency,
Notre Dame de Cléry,
Vendôme, Vendôme !

The Chimes of Vendôme
(English Translation)

My friends, what's left
For a Dauphin* prince who is so nice?
Orléans, Beaugency,
Notre Dame de Cléry,
Vendôme, Vendôme !

Notes

*The heir of France's throne is called the Dauphin, usually it's the king's eldest son.

Comments

"*The author of the Carillon de Vendôme song isn't known. There is an **interesting article in French** (http://www.vallee-du-loir.com/offices/vendome/page.asp?s=3&o=5&a=119) from Vendôme's tourist board that talks about it.*" -Monique

For more about Le carillon de Vendôme, go to:
http://www.mamalisa.com/?t=es&p=1782.

There, you'll find sheet music, an MP3 tune, a MIDI melody and a video performance.

Le coq est mort (The Rooster Is Dead)

This song can be sung as a round.

Le coq est mort
(French Children's Song)

Le coq est mort, le coq est mort
Le coq est mort, le coq est mort
Il ne dira plus co-co-di, co-co-da
Il ne dira plus co-co-di, co-co-da
Coco cocodi cocodi, coda.

The Rooster Is Dead
(English Translation)

The rooster's dead, the rooster's dead,
The rooster's dead, the rooster's dead.

He'll no longer say cocodi, cocoda,
He'll no longer say cocodi, cocoda,
Coco cocodi cocodi, coda.

Notes

*This song originally comes from the German song "**Der Hahn ist tot**
(http://www.mamalisa.com/?t=es&p=2564&c=38)".*

Comments

Monique said, "When I was a teenager, we would sing an alternate, slangy version..."

*Le coq est mort, le coq est mort,
Il a crevé, on l'a bouffé,
Il ne dira plus cocodi, cocoda,
Il ne dira plus co-co-di, co-co-da
Coco cocodi cocodi, coda.*

A Singable English Translation

*The rooster's dead, the rooster's dead,
He croaked and we gobbled him up,
He'll no longer say cocodi, cocoda
He'll no longer say cocodi, cocoda
Coco cocodi cocodi, coda.*

For more about Le coq est mort, go to:
http://www.mamalisa.com/?t=es&p=2567.

There, you'll find sheet music, a MIDI melody and a video performance.

Le grand cerf (The Big Deer)

Le grand cerf
(French Rhyme)

1 Dans sa maison
2 Un grand cerf
3 Regardait
4 Par la fenêtre
5 Un lapin
6 Venir à lui
7 Et frapper ainsi
8 Cerf! Cerf!
9 Ouvre-moi
10 Ou le chasseur me tuera
11 Lapin, lapin
12 Entre et viens
13 Me serrer la main.

The Big Deer
(English Translation)

1. In his house
2. A big deer

3. Was looking
4. Out the window
5. A rabbit
6. Coming towards him,
7. Knocks like this:
8. Deer! Deer!
9. Open up for me
10. Or the hunter will kill me
11. Rabbit, rabbit,
12. Enter and come
13. Shake hands with me.

Game Instructions

Corresponding Gestures:

1. Draw a square with your hands.
2. Raise your hands above your head with your fingers spread out like deer antlers.
3. Shade your eyes with your hands.
4. Draw a square with your hands again.
5. Put your hands by each side of your head making rabbit ears.
6. Make a "come to me" gesture.
7. Mime knocking at the door.
8. Raise your hands above your head with your fingers spread out like deer antlers, then repeat the gesture.
9. Mime opening a door.
10. Mime the hunter aiming his gun.
11. Put your hands by each side of your head making rabbit ears again.
12. Make a "come to me" gesture.
13. Mime shaking hands.

Comments

Arnaud wrote, "We heard lately that line #6 wasn't 'venir à lui' (coming towards him) but 'venir à l'huis', an old French word for 'door' which explains why the rabbit then knocks".
The word "huis" is now obsolete and can only be heard in "à huis-clos" meaning "with closed door" about in-camera trials.

Update April 2011: Sylvie sent us a second verse that goes…

Quand ils furent en tête à tête
Le cerf lui fit grande fête
Et le chasseur tout marri*
Retourna chez lui
"Cerf, cerf, grand merci,
Le chasseur est loin d'ici!
- Lapin, lapin, réjouis-toi
Et reste chez moi."

English translation

*When they were head to head
The deer welcomed him warmly,
And the very saddened hunter
Went back home.
"Deer, deer, thanks so much,
The hunter is far away."
"Rabbit, rabbit, rejoice
And stay home with me."*

* marri is an outdated word meaning sorry, saddened, grieved.

For more about Le grand cerf, go to: **http://www.mamalisa.com/?t=es&p=148**.

There, you'll find sheet music, an MP3 tune, a MIDI melody and a video performance.

Lundi matin (On Monday Morning)

Lundi matin
(French Children's song)

Lundi matin,
L'emp'reur, sa femme et le p'tit prince
Sont venus chez moi
Pour me serrer la pince*
Comm' j'étais parti
Le p'tit prince a dit
Puisque c'est ainsi
Nous reviendrons mardi.

Mardi matin,
L'emp'reur, sa femme et le p'tit prince
Sont venus chez moi
Pour me serrer la pince
Comm' j'étais parti
Le p'tit prince a dit
Puisque c'est ainsi
Nous reviendrons mercredi.

Mercredi matin,
L'emp'reur, sa femme et le p'tit prince
Sont venus chez moi
Pour me serrer la pince
Comm' j'étais parti
Le p'tit prince a dit
Puisque c'est ainsi
Nous reviendrons jeudi.

Jeudi matin,
L'emp'reur, sa femme et le p'tit prince
Sont venus chez moi
Pour me serrer la pince
Comm' j'étais parti
Le p'tit prince a dit
Puisque c'est ainsi
Nous reviendrons vendredi.

Vendredi matin,
L'emp'reur, sa femme et le p'tit prince
Sont venus chez moi
Pour me serrer la pince
Comm' j'étais parti
Le p'tit prince a dit
Puisque c'est ainsi

Nous reviendrons samedi.

Samedi matin,
L'emp'reur, sa femme et le p'tit prince
Sont venus chez moi
Pour me serrer la pince
Comm' j'étais parti
Le p'tit prince a dit
Puisque c'est ainsi
Nous reviendrons dimanche.

Dimanche matin,
L'emp'reur, sa femme et le p'tit prince
Sont venus chez moi
Pour me serrer la pince
Comm' j'étais parti
Le p'tit prince a dit
Puisqu'il n'y est plus
Nous ne reviendrons plus.

On Monday Morning
(English Translation)

On Monday morning
The emperor, his wife and the little prince,
Came to my house
To shake my hand.
Since I had left,
The little prince said,
"Since this is how it is,
We'll come back on Tuesday."

On Tuesday morning
The emperor, his wife and the little prince,
Came to my house
To shake my hand.
Since I had left,
The little prince said,
"Since this is how it is,
We'll come back on Wednesday."

On Wednesday morning
The emperor, his wife and the little prince,
Came to my house
To shake my hand.
Since I had left,
The little prince said,
"Since this is how it is,
We'll come back on Thursday."

On Thursday morning
The emperor, his wife and the little prince,

Came to my house
To shake my hand.
Since I had left,
The little prince said,
"Since this is how it is,
We'll come back on Friday."

On Friday morning
The emperor, his wife and the little prince,
Came to my house
To shake my hand.
Since I had left,
The little prince said,
"Since this is how it is,
We'll come back on Saturday."

On Saturday morning
The emperor, his wife and the little prince,
Came to my house
To shake my hand.
Since I had left,
The little prince said,
"Since this is how it is,
We'll come back on Sunday."

On Sunday morning
The emperor, his wife and the little prince,
Came to my house
To shake my hand.
Since I had left,
The little prince said,
"Since he's not here anymore,
We won't come back again."

Notes

*Pince : Slang word for "hand". It's only used nowadays in the expression "serrer la pince" - meaning "to shake hands".

Comments

*There's a Kenyan song that's similar to this one in a Bantu language. The song's called "**Wakyumwa Katambanga** (http://www.mamalisa.com/?p=229&t=es&c=34)" ("Early Sunday Morning"). Dickson Ndambuki from Kenya recently confirmed that the two songs have the same tune. Click on the link to go to the MAMA LISA'S WORLD KENYA song page to see the Kenyan song.*

For more about Lundi matin, go to: **http://www.mamalisa.com/?t=es&p=140**.

There, you'll find sheet music, an MP3 tune and a MIDI melody.

Malbrough s'en va-t-en guerre (Marlborough Is Going to War)

Malbrough is the French name for the Duke of Marlborough. The Duke of Marlborough was John Churchill, an English general who fought against France under King Louis XIV. An interesting side note is that John Churchill was Winston Churchill's ancestor.

Malbrough s'en va-t-en guerre
(French Children's Song)

Malbrough s'en va-t-en guerre,
Mironton ton ton mirontaine,
Malbrough s'en va-t-en guerre,
Ne sait quand reviendra,
Ne sait quand reviendra,
Ne sait quand reviendra.

Il reviendra à Pâques,
Mironton ton ton mirontaine,
Il reviendra à Pâques,

Ou à la Trinité,
Ou à la Trinité,
Ou à la Trinité.

La Trinité se passe,
Mironton ton ton mirontaine,
La Trinité se passe,
Malbrough ne revient pas,
Malbrough ne revient pas,
Malbrough ne revient pas.

Madame à sa tour monte,
Mironton ton ton mirontaine,
Madame à sa tour monte,
Si haut qu'elle peut monter,
Si haut qu'elle peut monter,
Si haut qu'elle peut monter.

Elle voit venir un page,
Mironton ton ton mirontaine,
Elle voit venir un page,
Tout de noir habillé,
Tout de noir habillé,
Tout de noir habillé.

Ô page ô mon beau page,
Mironton ton ton mirontaine,
Ô page ô mon beau page,
Quell's nouvell's apportez ?
Quell's nouvell's apportez ?
Quell's nouvell's apportez ?

Aux nouvelles que j'apporte,
Mironton ton ton mirontaine,
Aux nouvelles que j'apporte,
Vos beaux yeux vont pleurer,
Vos beaux yeux vont pleurer,
Vos beaux yeux vont pleurer.

Monsieur Malbrough est mort,
Mironton ton ton mirontaine,
Monsieur Malbrough est mort,
Et mort et enterré,
Et mort et enterré,
Et mort et enterré.

J' l'ai vu porté en terre,
Mironton ton ton mirontaine,
J' l'ai vu porté en terre,
Par quatre-z-officiers,
Par quatre-z-officiers,
Par quatre-z-officiers.

L'un portait sa cuirasse,

Mironton ton ton mirontaine,
L'un portait sa cuirasse,
L'autre son bouclier,
L'autre son bouclier,
L'autre son bouclier.

L' troisième portait son sabre,
Mironton ton ton mirontaine,
L' troisième portait son sabre,
L' quatrième ne portait rien,
L' quatrième ne portait rien,
L' quatrième ne portait rien.

****

À l'entour de sa tombe,
Mironton ton ton mirontaine,
À l'entour de sa tombe,
Romarin l'on planta,
Romarin l'on planta,
Romarin l'on planta.

Sur la plus haute branche,
Mironton ton ton mirontaine,
Sur la plus haute branche,
Le rossignol chanta,
Le rossignol chanta,
Le rossignol chanta.

On vit voler son âme,
Mironton ton ton mirontaine,
On vit voler son âme,
À travers les lauriers,
À travers les lauriers,
À travers les lauriers.

Chacun mit ventre à terre,
Mironton ton ton mirontaine,
Chacun mit ventre à terre,
Et puis se releva,
Et puis se releva,
Et puis se releva,.

Pour chanter les victoires,
Mironton ton ton mirontaine,
Pour chanter les victoires,
Que Malbrough remporta,
Que Malbrough remporta,
Que Malbrough remporta.

La cérémonie faite,
Mironton ton ton mirontaine,
La cérémonie faite,
Chacun s'en fut coucher,

Chacun s'en fut coucher,
Chacun s'en fut coucher.

Les uns avec leurs femmes,
Mironton ton ton mirontaine,
Les uns avec leurs femmes,
Et les autres tout seuls,
Et les autres tout seuls,
Et les autres tout seuls.

Ce n'est pas qu'il en manque,
Mironton ton ton mirontaine,
Ce n'est pas qu'il en manque,
Car j'en connais beaucoup,
Car j'en connais beaucoup,
Car j'en connais beaucoup.

Des brunes et puis des blondes,
Mironton ton ton mirontaine,
Des brunes et puis des blondes,
Et des châtaignes aussi,
Et des châtaignes aussi,
Et des châtaignes aussi.

J' n'en dis pas davantage,
Mironton ton ton mirontaine,
J' n'en dis pas davantage,
Car en voilà-z-assez,
Car en voilà-z-assez,
Car en voilà-z-assez.

Marlborough Is Going to War
(English Translation)

Marlborough is going to war,
Mironton ton ton mirontaine,
Marlborough is going to war,
Doesn't know when he'll come back,
Doesn't know when he'll come back,
Doesn't know when he'll come back.

He'll come back for Easter,
Mironton ton ton mirontaine,
He'll come back for Easter,
Or for Trinity Sunday,
Or for Trinity Sunday,
Or for Trinity Sunday.

Trinity Sunday is over,
Mironton ton ton mirontaine,
Trinity Sunday is over,
Marlborough isn't back,

Marlborough isn't back,
Marlborough isn't back.

Her Ladyship goes up into her tower,
Mironton ton ton mirontaine,
Her Ladyship goes up into her tower,
As high up as she can,
As high up as she can,
As high up as she can.

She sees a page coming,
Mironton ton ton mirontaine,
She sees a page coming,
Dressed all in black,
Dressed all in black,
Dressed all in black.

O page, O my nice page,
Mironton ton ton mirontaine,
O page, O my nice page,
What news do you bring?
What news do you bring?
What news do you bring?

When hearing the news I bring,
Mironton ton ton mirontaine,
When hearing the news I bring,
Your beautiful eyes will cry,
Your beautiful eyes will cry,
Your beautiful eyes will cry,.

Lord Marlborough is dead,
Mironton ton ton mirontaine,
Lord Marlborough is dead,
And dead and buried,
And dead and buried,
And dead and buried.

I saw him buried,
Mironton ton ton mirontaine,
I saw him buried,
By four officers,
By four officers,
By four officers.

One was carrying his breastplate,
Mironton ton ton mirontaine,
One was carrying his breastplate,
The other his shield,
The other his shield,
The other his shield.

The third was carrying his saber,
Mironton ton ton mirontaine,

The third was carrying his saber,
The fourth was carrying nothing,
The fourth was carrying nothing,
The fourth was carrying nothing.

****

Around his grave,
Mironton ton ton mirontaine,
Around his grave,
They planted a rosemary tree,
They planted a rosemary tree,
They planted a rosemary tree.

On its highest branch,
Mironton ton ton mirontaine,
On its highest branch,
The nightingale sang,
The nightingale sang,
The nightingale sang.

His soul was seen flying,
Mironton ton ton mirontaine,
His soul was seen flying,
Through the laurels,
Through the laurels,
Through the laurels.

Everyone lay down upon the earth,
Mironton ton ton mirontaine,
Everyone lay down upon the earth,
And then got up again,
And then got up again,
And then got up again.

To sing of the victories,
Mironton ton ton mirontaine,
To sing of the victories,
That Marlborough won,
That Marlborough won,
That Marlborough won.

The ceremony done,
Mironton ton ton mirontaine,
The ceremony done,
Everyone went to bed,
Everyone went to bed,
Everyone went to bed.

Some with their wives,
Mironton ton ton mirontaine,
Some with their wives,
And others all alone,
And others all alone,

And others all alone.

It's not because there are only a few,
Mironton ton ton mirontaine
It's not because there are only a few,
Because I know there's a lot,
Because I know there's a lot,
Because I know there's a lot.

Dark-haired ones and blondes,
Mironton ton ton mirontaine,
Dark-haired ones and blondes,
And auburns too,
And auburns too,
And auburns too.

I'll say no more about it,
Mironton ton ton mirontaine,
I'll say no more about it,
For that's quite enough,
For that's quite enough,
For that's quite enough.

Notes

French people typically finish the song at the spot in the lyrics above where you see this symbol *********.

"The Duke of Marlborough didn't actually die in the battle of Malplaquet in 1709 as the song suggests." -Monique Palomares

Photos & Illustrations

Comments

*Monique wrote: "Looking for some deeper information about the song, I came across the book "**Notes pour l'histoire de la chanson** (http://www.archive.org/stream/notespourlhistoi00lesp#page/94/mode/2up)" by V. Lespy (Librairie de J.B. Dumoulin, Paris, 1861). The author Lespy starts the book with an anecdote about this song, that it has an Arabic origin –both the lyrics and the music. The Arabic version was about the feats of one Mambrou. It is believed that the soldiers of James I of Aragon and Louis IX of France (Saint Louis) probably brought the song back from the crusades in the 13th century. It's the legend of Mambrou that French King Louis 16th's son's nurse sang to him. Mambrou was changed to Malbrough at the end of the 18th century. If you know some French you can read the whole story at the link above."*

*The Spanish version is called "**Mambrú se fue a la guerra** (http://www.mamalisa.com/?t=es&p=551&c=71)". You can click the link to read it.*

*The tune to "**For He's a Jolly Good Fellow**
(http://mamalisa.com/?t=es&p=2415&c=23)" comes from this song.*

For more about Malbrough s'en va-t-en guerre, go to:
http://www.mamalisa.com/?t=es&p=186.

There, you'll find sheet music, an MP3 tune and a MIDI melody.

Maudit sois-tu carillonneur (Curse You Bell-ringer)

Maudit sois-tu carillonneur
(French Round)

Maudit sois-tu carillonneur,
Toi qui naquis pour mon malheur !*
Dès le point du jour à la cloche il s'accroche,
Et le soir encore carillonne plus fort.
Quand sonnera-t-on la mort du sonneur ?

Curse You Bell-ringer
(English Translation)

Curse you bell-ringer,
You whose birth was my misfortune!
From the break of day he hangs on the bell,
And in the evening he rings it even louder.
When will they ring it for the death of the bell-ringer?

Notes

* Alternate version "Que Dieu créa pour mon malheur" ("That God created for my misfortune").

Photos & Illustrations

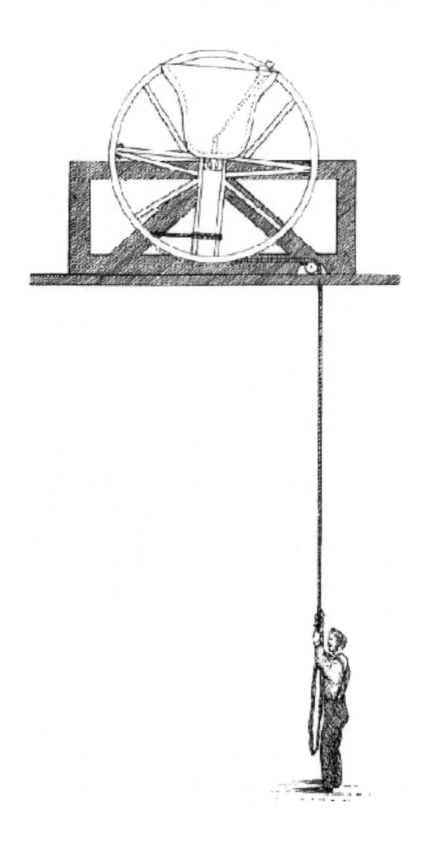

For more about Maudit sois-tu carillonneur, go to:
http://www.mamalisa.com/?t=es&p=3093.

There, you'll find sheet music, an MP3 tune and a MIDI melody.

Meunier, tu dors (Miller, You're Sleeping)

Meunier, tu dors
(French Children's Song)

Meunier tu dors
Ton moulin va trop vite
Meunier, tu dors
Ton moulin va trop fort.
Ton moulin, ton moulin va trop vite
Ton moulin, ton moulin va trop fort
Ton moulin, ton moulin va trop vite
Ton moulin, ton moulin va trop fort.

Miller, You're Sleeping
(English Translation)

Miller, you're sleeping,
Your mill spins too quickly
Miller, you're sleeping,
Your mill spins too strong.
Your mill, your mill spins too quickly,
Your mill, your mill spins too strong.
Your mill, your mill spins too quickly
Your mill, your mill spins too strong!

Notes

This song was traditionally sung as part of a circle dance.

Game Instructions

While singing the 1st four lines, the child turns his hands horizontally around each other. While singing the next two lines, he turns his hands very quickly forwards. While singing the last 2 lines, he turns his hands very quickly backwards.

For more about Meunier, tu dors, go to:
http://www.mamalisa.com/?t=es&p=163.

There, you'll find sheet music, an MP3 tune, a MIDI melody and a video performance.

Mon âne (My Donkey)

Mon âne
(French Children's Song)

Mon âne, mon âne
A bien mal à la têt',
Madam' lui a fait faire
Un bonnet pour sa fêt',
Un bonnet pour sa fêt',
Et des souliers oui-da, da, da
Et des souliers oui-da.*

Mon âne, mon âne
A bien mal aux oreill',
Madam' lui a fait fair'
Un' pair' de boucl's d'oreill'.
Un' pair' de boucl's d'oreill',
Un bonnet pour sa fêt',
Et des souliers oui-da, da, da
Et des souliers oui-da.

Mon âne, mon âne
A bien mal à ses yeux,
Madam' lui a fait fair'
Un' pair' de lunett's bleues.
Un' pair' de lunett's bleues,
Un' pair' de boucl's d'oreill',
Un bonnet pour sa fêt',

Et des souliers oui-da, da, da
Et des souliers oui-da.

Mon âne, mon âne
A bien mal à son nez,
Madam' lui a fait fair'
Un joli cache-nez.
Un joli cache-nez
Un' pair' de lunett's bleues,
Un' pair' de boucl's d'oreill',
Un bonnet pour sa fêt',
Et des souliers oui-da, da, da
Et des souliers oui-da.

Mon âne, mon âne
A bien mal à sa gorg',
Madam' lui a fait fair'
Un bâton d' sucre d'org'.
Un bâton d' sucre d'org,
Un joli ptit cach'-nez ,
Un' pair' de lunett's bleues:
Un' pair' de boucl's d'oreill',
Un bonnet pour sa fêt',
Et des souliers oui-da, da, da
Et des souliers oui-da.

Mon âne, mon âne
A mal à l'estomac,
Madam' lui a fait fair'
Un' tass' de chocolat.
Un' tass' de chocolat,
Un bâton d'sucre d'org',
Un joli cache-nez-
Un' pair' de lunett's bleues:
Un' pair' de boucl's d'oreill',
Un bonnet pour sa fêt',
Et des souliers oui-da, da, da
Et des souliers oui-da.

My Donkey
(English Translation)

My donkey, my donkey
Has a very bad headache.
The mistress had someone make for it
A bonnet for its name day**
A bonnet for its name day
And also shoes, oh yes, yes, yes,
And also shoes, oh yes.

My donkey, my donkey
Has a very bad earache.

The mistress had someone make for it
A pair of earrings,
A pair of earrings
A bonnet for its name day
And also shoes, oh yes, yes, yes,
And also shoes, oh yes.

My donkey, my donkey
Has very sore eyes.
The mistress had someone make for it
A pair of blue glasses,
A pair of blue glasses
A pair of earrings
A bonnet for its name day,
And also shoes, oh yes, yes, yes,
And also shoes, oh yes.

My donkey, my donkey
Has an ache on its nose,
The mistress had someone make for it
A pretty scarf,
A pretty scarf
A pair of blue glasses
A pair of earrings
A bonnet for its name day,
And also shoes, oh yes, yes, yes,
And also shoes, oh yes.

My donkey, my donkey
Has a very sore throat,
The mistress had someone make for it
A nice candy cane,
A nice candy cane
A pretty scarf
A pair of blue glasses
A pair of earrings
A bonnet for its name day,
And also shoes, oh yes, yes, yes,
And also shoes, oh yes.

My donkey, my donkey
Has a bad stomach ache,
The mistress had someone make for it
A cup of hot chocolate,
A cup of hot chocolate
A nice candy cane
A pretty scarf
A pair of blue glasses
A pair of earrings
A bonnet for its name day,
And also shoes, oh yes, yes, yes,
And also shoes, oh yes.

Notes

*"Oui-da" is an old popular expression in which "da" is an intensifier of "oui".
The most well-known version of this song doesn't go "et des souliers, oui-da" (and shoes, oh yes) but "et des souliers lilas" (and lilac colored shoes).
**Name Days are celebrated in Europe and South America. A person's name day is the Saint's Day of the Saint that the person was named after.

For more about Mon âne, go to: **http://www.mamalisa.com/?t=es&p=3012**.

There, you'll find sheet music, an MP3 tune and a MIDI melody.

Mon beau sapin (My Beautiful Fir Tree)

This is the French version of the German song "O Tannenbaum" (O Christmas Tree)...

Mon beau sapin
(French Christmas Song)

Mon beau sapin, roi des forêts
Que j'aime ta verdure!
Quand, par l'hiver, bois et guérets
Sont dépouillés de leurs attraits
Mon beau sapin, roi des forêts
Tu gardes ta parure.

Toi que Noël planta chez nous
Au saint anniversaire!
Comme ils sont beaux, comme ils sont doux
Et tes bonbons et tes joujoux!
Toi que Noël planta chez nous
Tout brillant de lumière.

Mon beau sapin tes verts sommets
Et leur fidèle ombrage
De la foi qui ne ment jamais
De la constance et de la paix,
Mon beau sapin tes verts sommets
M'offrent la douce image.

My Beautiful Fir Tree
(English Translation)

My beautiful fir tree, king of the forests
How much I like your leafy finery
When in Winter, woods and tilled land
Are bare of their appeal
My beautiful fir tree, king of the forests
You keep your leafy finery.

You that Christmas planted in our home
For the Holy Birthday
Pretty fir tree, how fine and
Sweet your candy and toys are,
You that Christmas planted in our home
All glittering.

My beautiful fir tree, your green treetops
And their loyal shading,
My beautiful fir tree, your green treetops
Give the sweet image
Of never-lying faith,
Of constancy and peace.

Notes

*This song is originally German. To read the German version go to **Mama Lisa's Germany page** (http://mamalisa.com/world/germany.html) and click on* O TANNENBAUM.

For more about Mon beau sapin, go to:
http://www.mamalisa.com/?t=es&p=164.

There, you'll find sheet music and a MIDI melody.

Nous n'irons plus au bois (We'll Go to the Woods No More)

These are traditional 18th century lyrics that are sung to the tune of the Gregorian Kyrie chant from "The Mass of the Angels".

Nous n'irons plus au bois
(French Circle Game Song)

Nous n'irons plus au bois,
Les lauriers sont coupés.
La belle que voilà,
La laiss'rons nous danser ? *

Refrain
Entrez dans la danse,
Voyez comme on danse,
Sautez, dansez,
Embrassez qui vous voudrez.

La belle que voilà,
La laiss'rons nous danser ? *
Et les lauriers du bois,
Les laiss'rons nous faner ?

(Refrain)

Non, chacune à son tour

Ira les ramasser.
Si la cigale y dort,
Ne faut pas la blesser.

(Refrain)

Le chant du rossignol
La viendra réveiller,
Et aussi la fauvette,
Avec son doux gosier.

(Refrain)

Et Jeanne, la bergère,
Avec son blanc panier,
Allant cueillir la fraise
Et la fleur d'églantier.

(Refrain)

Cigale, ma cigale,
Allons, il faut chanter
Car les lauriers du bois
Sont déjà repoussés.

We'll Go to the Woods No More
(English Translation)

We'll go to the woods no more,
The laurels have been cut.
That beauty there,
Will we let her dance?

(Chorus)
Join the dance
See how we dance,
Jump, dance,
Kiss whoever you want.

That beauty there,
Will we let her dance?
And the laurels in the woods
Will we let them wither?

(Chorus)

No, each one takes her turn
To go pick them.
If the cicada is sleeping there,
It must not be hurt.

(Chorus)

The song of the nightingale
Will wake it up,
And also the warbler
With its sweet voice.

(Chorus)

And Jean, the shepherdess
With her white basket,
Going to pick strawberries
And wild roses.

(Chorus)

Cicada, my cicada,
Come on, you must sing
For the laurels in the woods
Have grown again.

Notes

*Alternate line: "Ira les ramasser" (will go to pick them up).

Game Instructions

The children form a circle. One child is chosen to start the game. She's part of the circle with the others. "The beauty" is the child on her right. On the first verse, the children walk while singing. On "Entrez dans la danse" (Join the dance), "the beauty" goes to the center of the circle and dances. On the last line, she chooses someone and places her on her left. This child will be the next "beauty".

Comments

*At this link you can **hear a recording of this song** (http://gallica.bnf.fr/ark:/12148/bpt6k129161w) from 1930 at the BNF.*

For more about Nous n'irons plus au bois, go to:
http://www.mamalisa.com/?t=es&p=3456.

There, you'll find sheet music, a MIDI melody and a video performance.

Pirouette cacahuète (Pirouette Peanut Butter)

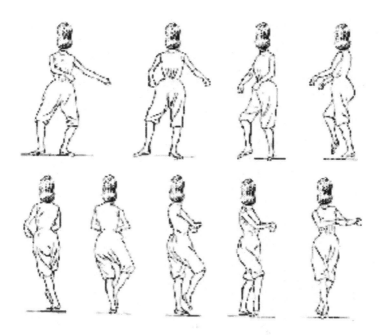

"Pirouette cacahuète" literally means "Pirouette Peanut". We translated it as "Pirouette Peanut Butter" so that you can sing the English version to the tune of the song.

Pirouette cacahuète
(French Children's Song)

Il était un petit homme,
Pirouette cacahuète,
Il était un petit homme,
Qui avait une drôle de maison,
Qui avait une drôle de maison.

Sa maison est en carton,
Pirouette cacahuète,
Sa maison est en carton,
Les escaliers sont en papier,
Les escaliers sont en papier.

Celui qui y montera,
Pirouette cacahuète,
Celui qui y montera,
Se cassera le bout du nez,
Se cassera le bout du nez.

Le facteur y est monté,
Pirouette cacahuète,
Le facteur y est monté,
Il s'est cassé le bout du nez,
Il s'est cassé le bout du nez.

On lui a raccommodé,
Pirouette cacahuète,
On lui a raccommodé,
Avec du joli fil doré,
Avec du joli fil doré.

Le joli fil a cassé,
Pirouette cacahuète,
Le joli fil a cassé,
Le bout du nez s'est envolé,
Le bout du nez s'est envolé.

Un avion à réaction,
Pirouette cacahuète,
Un avion à réaction,
A rattrapé le bout du nez,
A rattrapé le bout du nez.

Si mon histoire vous plaît,
Pirouette cacahuète,
Si mon histoire vous plaît,
Je peux vous la recommencer,
Je peux vous la recommencer.

OU
Mon histoire est terminée,
Pirouette cacahuète,
Mon histoire est terminée,
Messieurs, mesdames applaudissez,
Messieurs, mesdames applaudissez.

Pirouette Peanut Butter
(English Translation)

Once there was a little man
Pirouette peanut butter,
Once there was a little man
Who lived in quite a strange house,
Who lived in quite a strange house.

His strange house is made of cardboard
Pirouette peanut butter,
His strange house is made of cardboard
And the stairs are made of paper
And the stairs are made of paper.

Anyone who goes up them,
Pirouette peanut butter,
Anyone who goes up them,
Will break the tip of his nose,
Will break the tip of his nose.

The mailman, he went up them,
Pirouette peanut butter,
The mailman, he went up them,
He broke the tip of his nose,
He broke the tip of his nose.

He got his nose-tip mended,
Pirouette peanut butter,
He got his nose-tip mended,
With some pretty golden thread,
With some pretty golden thread.

But the pretty thread was broken,
Pirouette peanut butter,
But the pretty thread was broken,
And the nose-tip flew away,
And the nose-tip flew away.

A jet plane in the clear, blue sky,
Pirouette peanut butter,
A jet plane in the clear, blue sky,
Got the flying nose-tip back,
Got the flying nose-tip back.

If you really like my story,
Pirouette peanut butter,
If you really like my story,
I can sing it once again,
I can sing it once again.

OR
Now my story is finished,
Pirouette peanut butter,
Now my story is finished,
Ladies and gentlemen clap your hands,
Ladies and gentlemen clap your hands.

Notes

The translation is more or less singable!

For more about Pirouette cacahuète, go to:
http://www.mamalisa.com/?t=es&p=2180.

There, you'll find sheet music, an MP3 tune and a MIDI melody.

Pomme de reinette et pomme d'api (Pippin Apple and Lady Apple)

Pomme de reinette et pomme d'api
(French Children's Song)

Pomme de reinette et pomme d'api
Tapis, tapis rouge
Pomme de reinette et pomme d'api
Tapis, tapis gris.

Pippin Apple and Lady Apple
(English Translation)

Pippin apple and lady apple*,
Carpet, red carpet,
Pippin apple and lady apple,
Carpet, grey carpet.

Notes

*Lady apple (not Pink Lady) is one of the oldest varieties of apples.

Here's another version of this song that is sometimes used by French kids as a counting-out song (like the English rhyme EENIE, MEENIE, MINEY, MO).

Pomme de reinette et pomme d'api,
D'api, d'api rouge,
Pomme de reinette et pomme d'api,
D'api, d'api gris.
Cache ton poing derrière ton dos
Ou tu auras un coup d' marteau

Literal English Translation:

Pippin apple and lady apple,
Red, red lady apple,
Pippin apple and lady apple,
Grey, grey lady apple.
Hide your fist behind your back
Or you'll get a hammer blow.

Monique wrote, "I remember that we would add 'sorti!' (out!) at the end to eliminate one kid."

Comments

Recommended to sing while cooking a delicious **Tarte Tatin** (http://www.mamalisa.com/blog/?p=574)! (Click the link for more info.)

*****
Monique Palomares wrote the following about this song...

About the Name of the Apple and Where it Grew:

Pomme de reinette is a russet apple and pomme d'api has indeed no English translation: the apple was named "d'api" because it's said to have originated in a forest in Brittany called "forêt d'Apis" that no longer exists and that no longer existed when this variety of apples was first mentioned in print in 1628. Now... it may have existed but the author may not have known about it! Among the different varieties of api apples, there are red ones and grey ones, hence "d'api rouge" and "d'api gris", so the translation would be "red Api apple" and "gray Api apple".

The lyrics shifting from "d'api rouge" to "tapis rouge" (red carpet) is easily understandable if you consider that children aren't likely to know the names of fruit varieties when they (the fruit varieties) don't grow near where they live. Ditto for "pomm' de reinette". If I refer to my own experience, I grew up in a vineyard area and grapes had different names known to us kids while apples were only apples. Even now that I'm much older, pineapples are just pineapples, mangoes are just mangoes etc... though if you look at the **lyrics to the songs from where mangoes grow** (http://www.mamalisa.com/?t=es&p=2666&c=18)... it's much different in places where they grow. So... the song might have originated in Western France (Brittany, Normandy, Vendée) where the variety of apple was *probably known more than any other area.*

About the Tune:

In the book, COMPTINES DE LANGUE FRANÇAISE *(Seghers, Paris, 1961), the song is said to be found all over France + Belgium, Switzerland, Canada, La Réunion... There are many variants -even a "Spanish" one in Venezuela.*

One tune was first in print in 1821 in Paris, but it seems there are many tunes and that the song was already known before this tune was written down.

Monique's Experience with this Song:

When I was a child we used it as a counting-out rhyme and would add "Sorti!" at the end, splitting "sorti". The one on which "ti" fell went out and the song was repeated over and over again until there was only one left – that one was "It". We would also bounce a ball to the song -without "sorti". I also remember that for a looooong time this "pomm' de reinett' et pomm' d'api" was all Greek to us because our current version went "Pomparinett' et pontapi..." which is absolutely meaningless, and we also had the other lines as "tapis, tapis rouge" / "tapis, tapis gris".

For more about Pomme de reinette et pomme d'api, go to:
http://www.mamalisa.com/?t=es&p=1250.

There, you'll find sheet music, an MP3 tune and a MIDI melody.

Promenons-nous dans les bois (Let's Stroll in the Woods)

Promenons-nous dans les bois
(French Children's Song)

Promenons-nous dans les bois
Pendant que le loup n'y est pas
Si le loup y était
Il nous mangerait,
Mais comme il n'y est pas
Il n' nous mangera pas.
"Loup, y es-tu ?
Entends-tu ?
Que fais-tu ?"
"Je mets ma chemise !"

Promenons-nous dans les bois
Pendant que le loup n'y est pas
Si le loup y était
Il nous mangerait,
Mais comme il n'y est pas
Il n' nous mangera pas.
"Loup, y es-tu ?
Entends-tu ?
Que fais-tu ?"
"Je mets mes chaussettes !"

Promenons-nous dans les bois
Pendant que le loup n'y est pas
Si le loup y était
Il nous mangerait,
Mais comme il n'y est pas
Il n' nous mangera pas.
"Loup, y es-tu ?
Entends-tu ?
Que fais-tu ?"
"Je mets mon pantalon."

Promenons-nous dans les bois
Pendant que le loup n'y est pas
Si le loup y était
Il nous mangerait,
Mais comme il n'y est pas
Il n' nous mangera pas.
"Loup, y es-tu ?
Entends-tu ?
Que fais-tu ?"
"Je mets mes chaussures."

(On reprend le couplet autant de fois que le loup ajoute un vêtement/un accessoire : le chapeau, la veste, les lunettes… On finit par…)

Promenons-nous dans les bois
Pendant que le loup n'y est pas
Si le loup y était
Il nous mangerait,
Mais comme il n'y est pas
Il n' nous mangera pas.
"Loup, y es-tu ?
Entends-tu ?
Que fais-tu ?"
"Je prends mon fusil. J'arrive !"

Let's Stroll in the Woods
(English Translation)

Let's stroll in the woods
While the wolf is not here.
If the wolf was here
He would eat us,
But since he's not here
He won't eat us.
"Wolf, are you here?
Do you hear?
What are you doing?"
"I'm putting on my shirt!"

Let's stroll in the woods
While the wolf is not here.
If the wolf was here
He would eat us,
But since he's not here
He won't eat us.
"Wolf, are you here?
Do you hear?
What are you doing?"
"I'm putting on my socks!"

Let's stroll in the woods
While the wolf is not here.
If the wolf was here
He would eat us,
But since he's not here
He won't eat us.
"Wolf, are you here?
Do you hear?
What are you doing?"
"I'm putting on my pants!"

Let's stroll in the woods

While the wolf is not here.
If the wolf was here
He would eat us,
But since he's not here
He won't eat us.
"Wolf, are you here?
Do you hear?
What are you doing?"
"I'm putting on my shoes!"

The verse is sung as many times as needed while the wolf adds something, his hat, his jacket, his glasses, etc. It ends with...

Let's stroll in the woods
While the wolf is not here.
If the wolf was here
He would eat us,
But since he's not here
He won't eat us.
"Wolf, are you here?
Do you hear?
What are you doing?"
"I got my rifle. I'm coming!"

Game Instructions

One child is chosen to be the wolf. The children delineate a space. The child acting as the wolf stays hidden out of this space. While they sing the song, the children who "stroll" must walk inside the space. When the wolf comes out of his hiding spot, the "strollers" must run away without going out of the delineated space. The kids caught by the wolf must go and sit in the "house" of the wolf. The last one who hasn't been caught at the end becomes the new wolf. Then the game starts all over again.

Comments

In a minor variation of this song, the first part of each verse can be found without the first part of the negation (i.e. ne or n'). Informal French often doesn't use it. You can see this variation in the lines in italics below:

Promenons-nous dans les bois
PENDANT QUE LE LOUP Y EST PAS
Si le loup y était
Il nous mangerait,
MAIS COMME IL Y EST PAS
Il nous mangera pas.

For more about Promenons-nous dans les bois, go to:
http://www.mamalisa.com/?t=es&p=628.

There, you'll find sheet music, an MP3 tune and a MIDI melody.

Savez-vous planter les choux ? (Do You Know How to Plant Cabbage?)

Savez-vous planter les choux ?
(French Children's Song)

Savez-vous planter les choux
À la mode, à la mode ?
Savez-vous planter les choux
À la mode de chez nous ?

On les plante avec le doigt
À la mode, à la mode
On les plante avec le doigt
À la mode de chez nous.

On les plante avec les mains
À la mode, à la mode ?
On les plante avec les mains
À la mode de chez nous.

On les plante avec le pied
À la mode, à la mode ?
On les plante avec le pied
À la mode de chez nous.

On les plante avec le coude
À la mode, à la mode ?
On les plante avec le coude
À la mode de chez nous.

On les plante avec le nez
À la mode, à la mode ?
On les plante avec le nez
À la mode de chez nous.

Do You Know How to Plant Cabbage?
(English Translation)

Do you know how to plant cabbage
In the fashion, in the fashion,
Do you know how to plant cabbage
In the fashion of our country?

We plant them with the finger
In the fashion, in the fashion,
We plant them with the finger
In the fashion of our country.

We plant them with the hands
In the fashion, in the fashion,
We plant them with the hands
In the fashion of our country.

We plant them with the foot
In the fashion, in the fashion,
We plant them with the foot
In the fashion of our country.

We plant them with the elbow
In the fashion, in the fashion,
We plant them with the elbow
In the fashion of our country.

We plant them with the nose
In the fashion, in the fashion,
We plant them with the nose
In the fashion of our country.

Notes

More verses can be invented.

Game Instructions

First verse: Go around in a circle. Next verses: the children pretend to be planting with the part of the body that has been mentioned.

Photos & Illustrations

For more about Savez-vous planter les choux ?, go to:
http://www.mamalisa.com/?t=es&p=162.

There, you'll find sheet music, an MP3 tune and a MIDI melody.

46

Sur le plancher une araignée (A Spider on the Floor)

Sur le plancher une araignée
(French Nursery Rhyme)

Sur le plancher
Une araignée
Se tricotait des bottes
Dans un flacon
Un limaçon
Enfilait sa culotte
Je vois dans le ciel
Une mouche à miel
Pinçant sa guitare
Les rats tout confus
Sonnaient l'angélus
Au son de la fanfare.

A Spider on the Floor
(English Translation)

On the floor,
a spider
was knitting herself some boots.
In a bottle,
a snail
was pulling up its pants*.
In the sky, I see

a bee
plucking its guitar.
The rats, all confused,
were ringing the prayer bells**
to the sound of a brass band.

Notes

*"*Culotte*" meaning "trousers, pants or shorter breeches" is no longer in use. Nowadays, it only means girls' and women's underwear, which makes the children giggle.*

***Literally "Angelus" - which is a prayer said at morning, noon and night by Roman Catholics. A bell was traditionally rung at 6 am, noon and 6 pm to remind people to say this prayer. The bell rung was also called the "Angelus".*

Game Instructions

Each line is mimed.

For more about Sur le plancher une araignée, go to:
http://www.mamalisa.com/?t=es&p=149.

There, you'll find sheet music, an MP3 tune, a MIDI melody and a video performance.

Sur le pont d'Avignon (On the Bridge of Avignon)

My family and I visited the town of Avignon in France and took this photo of the Bridge of Avignon. Warning: If you visit there you won't be able to get the tune of this song out of your head for weeks!

Sur le pont d'Avignon
(French Children's Song)

Refrain
Sur le pont d'Avignon
On y danse, on y danse
Sur le pont d'Avignon
On y danse tout en rond*

1 Les beaux messieurs font comme ça
Et puis encore comme ça.

Refrain
Sur le pont d'Avignon
On y danse, on y danse
Sur le pont d'Avignon
On y danse tout en rond.

2 Les belles dames font comme ça
Et puis encore comme ça.

Refrain
Sur le pont d'Avignon

On y danse, on y danse
Sur le pont d'Avignon
On y danse tout en rond.

On the Bridge of Avignon
(English Translation)

(Chorus)
On the bridge of Avignon
They are dancing, they are dancing,
On the bridge of Avignon
They are dancing all around.

1. The handsome gentlemen go this way
And then again go that way.

(Chorus)
On the bridge of Avignon
They are dancing, they are dancing,
On the bridge of Avignon
They are dancing all around.

2. The pretty dames go this way
And then again go that way.

(Chorus)
On the bridge of Avignon
They are dancing, they are dancing,
On the bridge of Avignon
They are dancing all around.

Notes

*This line can be found as either "tout en rond" or "tous en rond".
"Tout en rond" means something like "in a circle". It sounds as if it's insisting on the fact that it's in a circle.
"Tous en rond" means "ALL in a circle". It means that EVERYBODY should dance on a circle.

Game Instructions

Children dance in a circle while singing the chorus. On the first verse, the dance stops and the children bow and pretend to raise their hats. On the second verse, the children curtsey first on one side and then on the other.

Photos & Illustrations

Comments

Monique wrote: "There are usually 2 verses to SUR LE PONT D'AVIGNON: *one about the gentlemen and the other about the ladies. In some versions, there's a verse about the shoemakers, and in other versions, there's quite a lot of people!*

I found the following people in my French song books, and online..."

Les cordonniers (shoemakers) font comme ça...
Les blanchisseuses (laundresses) font comme ça...
Les musiciens (musicians) font comme ça...
Les soldats (the soldiers) font comme ça...
Les jardiniers (gardeners) font comme ça...
Les vignerons (grape growers) font comme ça...
Les couturiers (dressmakers) font comme ça...

*****

Le pont d'Avignon is also called Pont Saint-Bénezet.

The tune to this song was in print as far back as 1853. The full song has been around in its current form since 1876.

Come visit MAMA LISA'S WORLD BLOG *to* **read more about the Bridge of Avignon and to see more photos** *(http://www.mamalisa.com/blog/?p=684).*

For more about Sur le pont d'Avignon, go to:
http://www.mamalisa.com/?t=es&p=155.

There, you'll find sheet music, an MP3 tune and a MIDI melody.

48

Sur le pont du Nord (On the North Bridge)

Sur le pont du Nord
(French Children's Song)

Sur le pont du Nord un bal y est donné
Sur le pont du Nord un bal y est donné

Adèle demande à sa mère d'y aller
Adèle demande à sa mère d'y aller

"Non, non ma fille tu n'iras pas danser"
"Non, non ma fille tu n'iras pas danser"

Monte à sa chambre et se met à pleurer
Monte à sa chambre et se met à pleurer

Son frère arrive dans son bateau doré
Son frère arrive dans son bateau doré

"Ma sœur, ma sœur qu'as-tu donc à pleurer"
"Ma sœur, ma sœur qu'as-tu donc à pleurer"

"Maman n' veut pas que j'aille au bal danser"
"Maman n' veut pas que j'aille au bal danser"

"Mets ta robe blanche et ta ceinture dorée"
"Mets ta robe blanche et ta ceinture dorée"

Le pont s'écroule et les voilà noyés
Le pont s'écroule et les voilà noyés

Voilà le sort des enfants obstinés
Voilà le sort des enfants obstinés.

On the North Bridge
(English Translation)

On the North Bridge a dance is given.
On the North Bridge a dance is given.

Adele asks her mother if she can go to it.
Adele asks her mother if she can go to it.

"No, no, my daughter, you will not go to dance."
"No, no, my daughter, you will not go to dance."

She goes up to her room and starts to cry.
She goes up to her room and starts to cry.

Her brother arrives in his golden boat.
Her brother arrives in his golden boat.

"Sister, sister, what are you crying about?"
"Sister, sister, what are you crying about?"

"Mommy doesn't want me to go to the dance."
"Mommy doesn't want me to go to the dance."

"Put on your white dress and your golden belt."
"Put on your white dress and your golden belt."

The bridges collapses and they drowned.
The bridges collapses and they drowned.

See the fate of obstinate children.
See the fate of obstinate children.

Comments

Monique sent alternate versions of this song:

"*Some versions have it as the Nantes Bridge (le pont de Nantes) instead of the North Bridge. The Nantes Bridge is in the French city of Nantes at the mouth of the Loire River.*

Some versions have the girl's name as 'Hélène' (Helen) instead of 'Adèle' (Adele), and the second line as, 'La belle Hélène voudrait bien y aller' (The beautiful Helen wanted to go to it).

Some versions have the lines below before the last line. This is the version I learned as a child:

Toutes les cloches se mirent à sonner
(All the bells started ringing)

La mère demande 'Qu'a-t-on à tant sonner ?' OU 'ce qu'elles ont à sonner'
(The mother asks, 'Why do they ring the bells so much?' OR 'For whom do they ring?')

'C'est pour Hélène et votre fils aîné'
(It's for Helen and your eldest son.)"

For more about Sur le pont du Nord, go to:
http://www.mamalisa.com/?t=es&p=3044.

There, you'll find sheet music, an MP3 tune and a MIDI melody.

Trois jeunes tambours (Three Young Drummers)

This song follows a pattern that's repeated for each verse: The first line is sung twice, followed by phrase, "And ri and ran, rapataplan, Were coming back from war."

Here we present the full first verse. For subsequent verses, we only present the first line.

Trois jeunes tambours
(French Children's Song)

Trois jeunes tambours s'en revenaient de guerre
Trois jeunes tambours s'en revenaient de guerre
Et ri et ran, rapataplan
S'en revenaient de guerre

Le plus jeune a dans sa bouche une rose

La fille du roi était à sa fenêtre

Joli tambour donne-moi donc ta rose

Fille du roi, donnez-moi votre cœur

Joli tambour, demand'-le à mon père

Sire le roi, donnez-moi votre fille

Joli tambour, tu n'es pas assez riche

J'ai trois vaisseaux dessus la mer jolie

L'un chargé d'or, l'autre de pierreries

Et le troisième pour promener ma mie

Joli tambour, dis-moi quel est ton père

Sire le roi, c'est le roi d'Angleterre

Joli tambour, je te donne ma fille

Sire le roi, je vous en remercie

Dans mon pays, il y en a d'aussi jolies.
(OU Dans mon pays, il y en a de plus jolies.)

Three Young Drummers
(English Translation)

Three young drummers were coming back from war,
Three young drummers were coming back from war,
And ri and ran, rapataplan,
Were coming back from war.

The youngest had a rose in his mouth...

The king's daughter was leaning out her window...

Nice drummer, give me your rose...

King's daughter, give me your heart...

Nice drummer, ask my father for it...

Your majesty, give me your daughter...

Nice drummer, you're not rich enough...

I've got three vessels out on the good sea...

One loaded with gold, the other with jewels...

And the third one is to take my sweetheart out...

Nice drummer, tell me who your father is...

Your majesty, it's the King of England...

Nice drummer, I give you my daughter...

Your majesty, I thank you very much for it...

In my country, there are girls just as pretty...
(OR In my country, there are prettier girls.)...

Notes

In French, "rapataplan" is the sound that drums make, the way "rat-a-tat-tat" represents the sound of drums in English.

For more about Trois jeunes tambours, go to:
http://www.mamalisa.com/?t=es&p=138.

There, you'll find sheet music, an MP3 tune and a MIDI melody.

50

Trois petits chats (Three Little Cats)

Trois petits chats
(French Handclapping Song)

Trois petits chats
Trois petits chats
Trois petits chats, chats, chats

Chapeau de paille
Chapeau de paille
Chapeau de paille, paille, paille

Paillasson,
Paillasson
Paillasson, son, son

Somnambule,

Somnambule,
Somnambule, -bule, -bule

Bulletin
Bulletin
Bulletin –tin, -tin

Tintamarre,
Tintamarre
Tintamarre, -marre, -marre

Marabout,
Marabout,
Marabout – bout, -bout,

Bout de ficelle
Bout de ficelle,
Bout de ficelle, -celle –celle

Selle de cheval
Selle de cheval
Selle de cheval –val, -val

Cheval de course,
Cheval de course,
Cheval de course, course, course

Course à pied,
Course à pied
Course à pied, pied, pied

Pied à terre,
Pied à terre
Pied à terre, terre, terre

Terre de feu
Terre de feu
Terre de feu, feu, feu

Feu follet
Feu follet
Feu follet –let – let

Lait de vache
Lait de vache
Lait de vache, vache, vache

Vache de ferme
Vache de ferme
Vache de ferme, ferme, ferme

Ferme ta gueule
Ferme ta gueule
Ferme ta gueule, gueule, gueule

Gueule de loup
Gueule de loup
Gueule de loup, loup, loup

Loup des bois
Loup des bois
Loup des bois, bois, bois

Boîte aux lettres
Boîte aux lettres
Boîte aux lettres, lettres, lettres

Lettres d'amour
Lettres d'amour
Lettres d'amour –mour, -mour

'mour à trois
'mour à trois
'mour à trois, trois, trois

Trois petits chiens
Trois petits chiens
Trois petits chiens, chiens, chiens

Chien de garde,
Chien de garde,
Chien de garde, garde, garde

Garde à vous,
Garde à vous
Garde à vous, vous, vous

Vous voulez,
Vous voulez
Vous voulez, -lez, -lez

Lait de vache
Lait de vache
Lait de vache, vache, vache…

Three Little Cats
(English Translation)

Three little cats,
Three little cats,
Three little cats, cats, cats.

Straw hat,
Straw hat,
Straw hat, hat, hat.

Doormat,
Doormat,
Doormat, mat, mat.

Sleepwalker,
Sleepwalker,
Sleepwalker, -ker, –ker.

Bulletin,
Bulletin,
Bulletin, –tin, -tin.

Big ruckus,
Big ruckus,
Big ruckus, -kus, -kus.

Marabout,
Marabout,
Marabout, –bout, -bout.

Piece of string,
Piece of string,
Piece of string, string, string.

Horse saddle,
Horse saddle,
Horse saddle, -dle, -dle.

Racing horse,
Racing horse,
Racing horse, horse, horse.

Foot race,
Foot race,
Foot race, race, race.

Foot on the ground, (1)
Foot on the ground,
Foot on the ground, ground, ground.

Land of fire, (2)
Land of fire,
Land of fire, fire, fire.

Will o' the wisp,
Will o' the wisp,
Will o' the wisp, wisp, wisp.

Cow's milk,
Cow's milk,
Cow's milk, milk, milk.

Farm cow,
Farm cow,

Farm cow, cow, cow.

Shut your mouth, (3)
Shut your mouth,
Shut your mouth, mouth, mouth.

Wolf's mouth, (4)
Wolf's mouth,
Wolf's mouth, mouth, mouth.

Woodland wolf,
Woodland wolf,
Woodland wolf, wolf, wolf.

Mailbox,
Mailbox,
Mailbox, box, box.

Love letter,
Love letter,
Love letter, -ter, -ter.

Love between three,
Love between three,
Love between three, three, three.

Three little dogs,
Three little dogs,
Three little dogs, dogs, dogs.

Guard dog,
Guard dog,
Guard dog, dog, dog.

Stand at attention,
Stand at attention,
Stand at attention, -tion, -tion.

You want,
You want,
You want, want, want.

Cow's milk,
Cow's milk,
Cow's milk, milk, milk...

Notes

(1) A "Pied à terre" is both a French and an English term meaning secondary lodging. But it also literally means "foot to the ground" in French.
(2) This can literally be translated as "Land of fire", or it can refer to the "Tierra del Fuego" which is a group of islands off the southern tip of South America.

(3) Note: "Ferme ta gueule" is rude because "gueule" is the word used to formally mean animals' mouths (i.e. snouts). It's used mostly for dogs, wolves, lions, tigers, etc... So to say "Ferme ta gueule" to a human being is considered rude. (Of course kids sing "Ferme ta gueule" because it's the rude way to say it, so it's much more exciting!)
(4) This can be either three separate French words, "gueule de loup" meaning "wolf's mouth" or it can be the compound word "gueule-de-loup" which refers to a "snapdragon" flower.

Photos & Illustrations

Comments

Since the structure of French is different from English, i.e. the qualifier goes AFTER the qualified word rather than BEFORE it, you can't perfectly translate this type of rhyme.

Manuela sent us a shorter version of the song with a slight difference after the "foot race" verse:

*Course à pied (foot race),
Course à pied
Course à pied, pied, pied*

Pied de cochon (PIG FOOT)
*Pied de cochon
Pied de cochon, -chon, -chon*

Cochon de ferme (FARM PIG)
*Cochon de ferme
Cochon de ferme, ferme, ferme…*

For more about Trois petits chats, go to:
http://www.mamalisa.com/?t=es&p=1441.

There, you'll find an MP3 tune.

Un éléphant, ça trompe (One Elephant That Deceives)

This song is a wordplay based on ça trompe meaning "it deceives" and sa trompe meaning "its trunk". Both phrases sound the same.

Un éléphant, ça trompe
(French Children's Song)

Un éléphant, ça trompe, ça trompe,
Un éléphant, ça trompe énormément.

Deux éléphants, ça trompe, ça trompe,
Deux éléphants, ça trompe énormément.

Trois éléphants, ça trompe, ça trompe,
Trois éléphants, ça trompe énormément

La peinture à l'huile
C'est bien difficile
Mais c'est bien plus beau
Que la peinture à l'eau.

Oléo oh oh, léo léo oh oh,
Oléo oh oh, léo léo oh oh,

Oléo oh oh, léo léo oh oh,
Oléo oh oh, léo léo.

One Elephant That Deceives
(English Translation)

One elephant that deceives, that deceives,
One elephant that deceives enormously.

Two elephants that deceive, that deceive,
Two elephants that deceive enormously.

Three elephants that deceive, that deceive,
Three elephants that deceive enormously.

Oil painting
Is very difficult
But it's much more lovely
Than watercolor painting.

Olay oh oh, olay olay oh oh oh,
Olay oh oh, olay olay oh oh oh,
Olay oh oh, olay olay oh oh oh,
Olay oh oh, olay olay oh.

Notes

HERE'S A TRANSLATION BY LISA THAT FITS THE TUNE:

One elephant, that tricks us, that tricks us,
One elephant tricks us enormously.

Two elephants that trick us, that trick us,
Two elephants trick us enormously.

Three elephants that trick us, that trick us,
Three elephants trick us enormously.

HERE'S A RHYMING VERSION BY MONIQUE:

An elephant deceives you, deceives you,
An elephant deceives you and others too.

Two elephants deceive you, deceive you,
Two elephants deceive you and others too.

Three elephants deceive you, deceive you,
Three elephants deceive you and others too...

For more about Un éléphant, ça trompe, go to:
http://www.mamalisa.com/?t=es&p=3068.

There, you'll find sheet music, an MP3 tune and a MIDI melody.

Un éléphant se balançait (One Elephant was Swinging on a Spider Web)

In this song, the elephants are swinging on a spider web as if they're on a swing.

You can sing the English translation to the tune if you sing the word "swinging" using 3 beats like "swin-nnnng-ing".

Un éléphant se balançait
(French Children's Song)

Un éléphant se balançait
Sur une toile, toile, toile, toile d'araignée,
C'était un jeu tellement amusant
Qu'il appela... un deuxième éléphant

Deux éléphants se balançaient
Sur une toile, toile, toile, toile d'araignée,
C'était un jeu tellement amusant
Qu'ils appelèrent... un troisième éléphant

Trois éléphants se balançaient
Sur une toile, toile, toile, toile d'araignée,

C'était un jeu tellement amusant
Qu'ils appelèrent... un quatrième éléphant

Quatre éléphants se balançaient
Sur une toile, toile, toile, toile d'araignée,
C'était un jeu tellement amusant
Qu'ils appelèrent... un cinquième éléphant

Cinq éléphants se balançaient
Sur une toile, toile, toile, toile d'araignée,
C'était un jeu tellement amusant
Que tout d'un coup... BaDaBouM !

One Elephant was Swinging on a Spider Web
(English Translation)

One elephant was swinging
On a web, web, web, a spider's web,
It was such a fun game, so much fun
That he called.... a second elephant.

Two elephants were swinging
On a web, web, web, a spider's web,
It was such a fun game, so much fun
That they called... a third elephant.

Three elephants were swinging
On a web, web, web, a spider's web,
It was such a fun game, so much fun
That they called... a fourth elephant.

Four elephants were swinging
On a web, web, web, a spider's web,
It was such a fun game, so much fun
That they called... a fifth elephant.

Five elephants were swinging
On a web, web, web, a spider's web,
It was such a fun game, so much fun
That suddenly... Badaboum!

Notes

The line "C'était un jeu tellement amusant" translates more literally to "It was a game that was so much fun." I changed it to fit the tune in the mp3.

The standard lyrics to this song are slightly different:

Un éléphant se balançait
sur une toile d'araignée,

il trouva ça si amusant,
qu'il appela un autre éléphant.

Deux éléphants se balançaient etc. etc.

English Translation:

An elephant was swinging
On a spider's web,
He found it so fun
He called another elephant.

Two elephants were swinging etc. etc.

For more about Un éléphant se balançait, go to:
http://www.mamalisa.com/?t=es&p=2221.

There, you'll find an MP3 tune and a MIDI melody.

Un kilomètre à pied ça use, ça use (One Kilometer on Foot Wears Out Your Shoes for Good)

All French-speaking children know this march-song.

Un kilomètre à pied ça use, ça use
(French Children's Song)

Un kilomètre à pied ça use, ça use,
Un kilomètre à pied ça use les souliers.

Deux kilomètres à pied ça use, ça use,
Deux kilomètres à pied ça use les souliers... etc.

One Kilometer on Foot Wears Out Your Shoes for Good
(English Translation)

One kilometer on foot wears out, wears out,
One kilometer on foot wears out your shoes for good.

Two kilometers on foot, wears out, wears out,
Two kilometers on foot, wears out your shoes for good... etc.

Comments

Lucie Lasseel sent us a more complete version:

Un kilomètre à pied, ça use, ça use
Un kilomètre à pied, ça use les souliers.
La peinture à l'huile c'est bien difficile
mais c'est bien plus beau
que la peinture à l'eau

Deux kilomètres à pied etc....

English Translation

One kilometer on foot wears out, wears out,
One kilometer on foot wears out your shoes for good.
Oil painting's not easy it would drive you crazy*
But it is more fine than watercolor lines.

*Literally:
Oil painting is very difficult
But it's more beautiful
Than watercolor painting.

*****

Harald Meilicke wrote, "I know a variant that goes on, instead of the verse 'la peinture a l'huile', like this:

Le café trop sucré donne la colique
Le café trop sucré donne mal aux pieds

(Coffee too sweetened gives a stomachache
Coffee too sweetened makes the feet hurt.)

However, it must be a different melody than la peinture a l'huile, whose melody I don't know."

For more about Un kilomètre à pied ça use, ça use, go to:
http://www.mamalisa.com/?t=es&p=2451.

There, you'll find sheet music, a MIDI melody and a video performance.

Un petit cochon (A Little Pig)

This rhyme is for choosing who will be "It".

Un petit cochon
(French Counting-out Rhyme)

Un petit cochon
Pendu au plafond
Tirez-lui le nez
Il donn'ra du lait
Tirez-lui la queue
Il pondra des œufs
Tirez-la plus fort
Il pondra de l'or
Combien en voulez-vous ?

A Little Pig
(English Translation)

A little pig
Hanging from the ceiling,
Pull its nose
It will give some milk,
Pull its tail
It will lay some eggs,
Pull it harder
It will lay some gold.
How much do you want?

Notes

The version of the rhyme above includes all the lines that can be found for it. The usual short version goes:

*Un petit cochon
Pendu au plafond
Tirez-lui la queue
Il pondra des œufs
Combien en voulez-vous ?*

English Translation :

*A little pig
Hanging from the ceiling
Pull its tail
It will lay some eggs
How many of them do you want?*

Photos & Illustrations

For more about Un petit cochon, go to:
http://www.mamalisa.com/?t=es&p=146.

There, you'll find sheet music and a MIDI melody.

Un, deux, trois, nous allons au bois (One, Two, Three, We Are Going into the Woods)

"This is a song I learnt from my French grandmother. She taught it to us as children, and we used to sing it as we marched together on woodland walks. Many happy memories." –Eleanor Blaxband Ashby

Un, deux, trois, nous allons au bois
(French Children's Song)

Un, deux, trois,
nous allons au bois.
Quatre, cinq, six,
cueillir des cerises.
Sept, huit, neuf,
dans un panier neuf.
Dix, onze, douze,
elles seront toutes rouges.

One, Two, Three, We Are Going into the Woods
(English Translation)

One, two, three,
We are going into the woods.
Four, five, six,
To pick some cherries.
Seven, eight, nine,
(we will put them) in a new basket.
Ten, eleven, twelve,
They will be all red.

For more about Un, deux, trois, nous allons au bois, go to:
http://www.mamalisa.com/?t=es&p=3193.

There, you'll find sheet music, a MIDI melody and a video performance.

56

Une poule sur un mur (A Hen on a Wall)

Une poule sur un mur
(French Nursery Rhyme)

Une poule sur un mur
Qui picote du pain dur
Picoti, picota
Lève la queue
Et puis s'en va.

A Hen on a Wall
(English Translation)

A hen on a wall
Pecking some dry bread
Pecky, peckay
Raises her tail
Then goes away.

For more about Une poule sur un mur, go to:
http://www.mamalisa.com/?t=es&p=147.

There, you'll find sheet music, an MP3 tune and a MIDI melody.

Une souris verte (A Green Mouse)

Une souris verte
(French Nursery Rhyme)

Une souris verte
Qui courait dans l'herbe.
Je l'attrape par la queue,
Je la montre à ces messieurs.
Ces messieurs me disent :
Trempez-la dans l'huile,
Trempez-la dans l'eau,
Ça fera un escargot
Tout chaud.
Je la mets dans un tiroir,
Elle me dit : Il fait trop noir.
Je la mets dans mon chapeau,
Elle me dit : Il fait trop chaud.

A Green Mouse
(English Translation)

A green mouse
That ran in the grass,
I caught it by its tail
I showed it to those men.

The men said:
Dip it in oil,
Dip it in water
It will become a snail
Nice and warm.
I put it in a draw
It told me, "It's too dark."
I put it in my hat
It told me, "It's too warm."

Notes

Usually there are two other lines that go:

Je la mets dans ma culotte*
Elle me fait trois petites crottes.

ENGLISH TRANSLATION:

I put it in my pants
It makes three little droppings.

*CULOTTE USED TO MEAN PANTS OR BREECHES, NOWADAYS IT'S THE WORD FOR LADIES' UNDERWEAR.

Another version after "un escargot tout chaud" goes:

Qui est la marraine
Une sauterelle
Qui est le parrain
C'est un gros lapin.

Elle monte à sa chambre
Se casse une jambe
Elle monte au grenier
Elle se casse le bout du nez.

ENGLISH TRANSLATION:

Who's the godmother,
A grasshopper.
Who's the godfather,
It's a big rabbit.

She goes up to her bedroom,
Breaks her leg,
She goes up to the attic,
She breaks the tip of her nose.

*****

Update, April 2011. Sylvie wrote, "A suggestion for this poor green mouse that doesn't feel comfy anywhere! It's to the usual tune…

Je la mets dans mon tiroir
elle me dit qu'il fait trop noir
je la mets dans mon chapeau
elle me dit qu'il fait trop chaud
je la mets dans ma chemise
elle me fait 3 petites bises
(et on compte bien sûr les 3 bises : tout est prétexte!!!)
je la mets dans ma culotte
elle me fait 3 petites crottes
(idem : prout prout prout!)
je la mets dans une casserole
elle me danse le rock&roll
(bruits de pieds ad libitum, et les enfants ne s'en privent pas! mais on revient vite au calme)

English translation of this first part…

I put her in my drawer
She tells me it's too dark,
I put her in my hat,
She tells me it's too hot,
I put her in my shirt,
She gives me three little kisses
(and we of course count the kisses: everything is a pretext to mime something)
I put her in my trousers
She makes three little droppings
(ditto: poot poot poot!)
I put her in a saucepan,
She dances the rock & roll
(Make noise with feet ad infinitum, the children enjoy it, but are soon requested to quiet down.)

…I invented a sequel with children some years ago. Here it is: you open your hand and you caress the mouse, be careful, very softly and with only one finger to avoid hurting her!

Je la pose dans ma main
je lui fait un p'tit câlin
elle me dit :"je suis très bien!"
(Petit geste de contentement de la souris blottie sur la dernière phrase et ralenti "elle me dit je - suis- très--bien!".)

English translation of the end:

I lay her in my hand
I give her a little cuddle
She tells me "I feel very good".
(Little gesture of being made pleased by the "cuddled mouse" on the last sentence and slow down the tempo "she tells me I - feel - very - good".)

Something had to be done for this poor green mouse that suffered so many problems, hadn't it?

For more about Une souris verte, go to:
http://www.mamalisa.com/?t=es&p=144.

There, you'll find sheet music, an MP3 tune and a MIDI melody.

Vent frais, vent du matin (Fresh Wind, Morning Wind)

This is a round for 3 voices.

The English translation can be sung to the tune.

Vent frais, vent du matin
(French Round)

Vent frais, vent du matin,
soulevant le sommet des grands pins,
joie du vent qui souffle*, allons dans le grand...

Vent frais, vent du matin,
soulevant le sommet des grands pins,

joie du vent qui souffle, allons dans le grand...

Vent frais, vent du matin,
soulevant le sommet des grands pins,
joie du vent qui souffle, allons dans le grand vent.

Fresh Wind, Morning Wind
(English Translation)

Wind, fresh, wind of the morn,
Lifting the treetops of the great pines,
Joyful blowing wind, let's walk in the great...

Wind, fresh, wind of the morn,
Lifting the treetops of the great pines,
Joyful blowing wind, let's walk in the great...

Wind, fresh, wind of the morn,
Lifting the treetops of the great pines,
Joyful blowing wind, let's walk in the great wind.

Notes

*Or "passe" in French.

*****

Another Version:

Vent frais, vent du matin
Vent qui souffle au sommet des grands pins
Joie du vent qui souffle, allons dans le grand...

Vent frais, vent du matin
Vent qui souffle au sommet des grands pins
Joie du vent qui souffle, allons dans le grand...

Vent frais, vent du matin
Vent qui souffle au sommet des grands pins
Joie du vent qui souffle, allons dans le grand vent.

ENGLISH TRANSLATION:

Fresh wind, morning wind,
Wind that blows the tops of the tall pines
Joy of wind that blows, let's go out in the strong...

Fresh wind, morning wind,
Wind that blows the tops of the tall pines
Joy of wind that blows, let's go out in the strong...

Fresh wind, morning wind,
Wind that blows the tops of the tall pines
Joy of wind that blows, let's go out in the strong wind.

For more about Vent frais, vent du matin, go to:
http://www.mamalisa.com/?t=es&p=3234.

There, you'll find sheet music, a MIDI melody and a video performance.

Thanks and Acknowledgements!

We're so grateful to everyone who helped us gather the material for this book. And special thanks to Mama Lisa's daughter and her friends for their wonderful drawings.

Merci!

1 À cheval sur mon bidet (Riding My Horsey)
Many thanks to Stéphane Jourdan for sharing his family's version!

Image from "ABC of Fox Hunting" by Sir John Dean Paul, edited by Mama Lisa.

2 À déli délo (Ah Deli Delo)
Translation by Monique and Lisa. Thanks to Lila Pomerantz for the drawing.

3 À la claire fontaine (At the Clear Spring)
Many thanks to Jade Kite for contributing this song and to Monique Palomares for the midi music and for the photos of the spring in Croatia. Translation by Monique Palomares and Lisa Yannucci.

4 Ah ! Mon beau château ! (Oh! My Beautiful Castle!)
Many thanks to **Edit' Dupont** (http://www.editdupont.com) for contributing and singing this song for Mama Lisa's World. Thanks to Monique Palomares for the midi tune. Translated by Monique Palomares and Lisa Yannucci. Illustration from "Chansons et rondes enfantines" (1859) by Théophile Marion Dumersan and Gustave Jeane-Julien.

5 Ah ! Vous dirai-je Maman (Oh! Shall I Tell You Mommy)
Many thanks to Monique Palomares for contributing this song and creating the midi music. Translation by Lisa and Monique.

Illustration by Louis-Maurice Boutet de Monvel (1851-1913) from VIEILLES CHANSONS POUR LES PETITS ENFANTS: AVEC ACCOMPAGNEMENTS / de Ch. M. Widor (1844 - 1937); Illustrations Par M.B. de Monvel. Paris: E. Plon, Nourrit et Cie, [1883]. The image was graphically edited by Lisa Yannucci.

6 Alouette, gentille alouette (Lark, Sweet Lark)

Many thanks to Monique Palomares for contributing this song, for the midi music and the score. Translated by Monique and Lisa.

7 Au clair de la lune (Under the Moonlight)
Many thanks to Elena for contributing the 1st two verses of this song and to Monique Palomares for contributing the missing verses and creating the midi music. Translation by Lisa Yannucci and Monique Palomares.

Illustration by Louis-Maurice Boutet de Monvel (1851-1913) from VIEILLES CHANSONS POUR LES PETITS ENFANTS: AVEC ACCOMPAGNEMENTS / de Ch. M. Widor (1844 - 1937); Illustrations par M.B. de Monvel. Paris: E. Plon, Nourrit et Cie, [1883]. The image was graphically edited by Lisa Yannucci.

The 2nd illustration is from CHANSONS ET RONDES ENFANTINES (1871) with a little graphical editing by Lisa Yannucci.

8 Au feu les pompiers (Fire! Firemen, Fire!)
Translation: Lisa Yannucci and Monique Palomares

9 Aux marches du palais (Down the Palace Stairs)
Many thanks to La Grande Bleue for contributing this song. **La Grande Bleue** (http://www.lgb.levillagemusical.fr/) is a group of musicians who mainly write and create songs and shows for children.

Translated by Monique Palomares and Lisa Yannucci.

11 C'est Gugusse (It's Gugusse)
Translation: Monique Palomares and Lisa Yannucci

12 Cadet Rousselle
Thanks to Monique Palomares for contributing this rhyme. Translation: Monique and Lisa.

Portrait of Cadet Rousselle is from a painting by Charles Dropy.

13 Compagnons de la Marjolaine (Company of the Marjoram)
Translated by Monique Palomares and Lisa Yannucci.

Image: "Le petit français illustré: journal des écoliers et des écolières", Volume 15, Issue 2 (1903).

14 Compère Guilleri (Fellow Guilleri)
Many thanks to Jade Kite for contributing this song. Translated by Monique Palomares and Lisa Yannucci.

Image: "Le petit français illustré: journal des écoliers et des écolières", Volume 15, Issue 2 (1903)

15 Dans la forêt lointaine (In the Faraway Forest)
Many thanks to Monique Palomares for contributing and translating this song and for creating the midi music. Thanks to Lila Pomerantz for the illustration!

16 Douce nuit (Sweet Night)
Literal English translation of the French version by Monique and Lisa.

17 Frère Jacques (Brother John)
Illustration by Louis-Maurice Boutet de Monvel (1851-1913) from VIEILLES CHANSONS POUR LES PETITS ENFANTS: AVEC ACCOMPAGNEMENTS / de Ch. M. Widor (1844 - 1937); Illustrations Par M.B. de Monvel. Paris: E. Plon, Nourrit et Cie, [1883]. The image was graphically edited by Lisa Yannucci.

18 Gentil coquelicot (Nice Poppy)
Many thanks to Monique Palomares for contributing this song and creating the midi and sheet music. Translation by Lisa and Monique

The 1st illustration is from "Les fleurs animées, Volume 1" (1847) by Gabriel de Gonet, with some graphical editing by Lisa Yannucci.

The 2nd illustration is from CHANSONS ET RONDES ENFANTINES (1871) with some graphical editing by Lisa Yannucci.

19 Il court le furet (The Ferret Runs)
Many thanks to Jade Kite for contributing this song and to Monique Palomares for the midi music!

Illustration by Louis-Maurice Boutet de Monvel (1851-1913) from VIEILLES CHANSONS POUR LES PETITS ENFANTS: AVEC ACCOMPAGNEMENTS / de Ch. M. Widor (1844 - 1937); Illustrations Par M.B. de Monvel. Paris: E. Plon, Nourrit et Cie, [191-]. The image was graphically edited by Lisa Yannucci.

20 Il était un petit navire (There Was a Little Ship)
Many thanks to Jade Kite for contributing this song and to Monique Palomares for the English translation.

Image: "Petit Larousse illustré: nouveau dictionnaire encyclopédique" (1906).

21 Il était une bergère (There Was a Shepherdess)
Many thanks to Monique Palomares for contributing and translating this song, and for providing the midi and sheet music. Thanks to Harald Meilicke for sharing an alternate ending.

The illustration is from CHANSONS ET RONDES ENFANTINES (1870).

22 Il était un' dame Tartine (There Was a Lady Slice of Bread)
Translation: Monique Palomares and Lisa Yannucci. Thanks to Lila Pomerantz for the illustration!

23 J'ai du bon tabac (I Have Good Tobacco)
Translated by Monique and Lisa.

24 J'ai perdu le do de ma clarinette (I Lost the C on My Clarinet)
Translation: Monique Palomares and Lisa Yannucci.

25 J'ai vu le loup, le renard, le lièvre (I Saw the Wolf, The Fox, The Hare)
Many thanks to Monique Palomares for contributing and translating this song and for creating the midi and the sheet music.

26 J'aime la galette (I Love Cake)
Thanks to Krisztina Szabo for helping with the lyrics.

27 Jean Petit qui danse (John Petit)
Many thanks to Monique Palomares for contributing this song, for the score and the midi. Translation by Monique and Lisa.

28 La bonne aventure ô gué (A Fine Adventure, Oh Joy!)
Many thanks to **Edit' Dupont** (http://www.editdupont.com) for contributing and singing this song for Mama Lisa's World. Translated by Monique Palomares and Lisa Yannucci.

29 La légende de Saint Nicolas (The Legend of Saint Nicholas)
Many thanks to Jade Kite for contributing this song. Translated by Monique and Lisa.

Image: "Les légendes de France" (1885) by Henry Carnoy.

30 La mère Michel (Old Ma Michel)
Many thanks to Jade Kite for contributing this song and to Monique Palomares for creating the midi music. Translation by Monique and Lisa.

Illustration by Louis-Maurice Boutet de Monvel (1851-1913) from VIEILLES CHANSONS POUR LES PETITS ENFANTS: AVEC ACCOMPAGNEMENTS / de Ch. M. Widor (1844 - 1937); Illustrations Par M.B. de Monvel. Paris: E. Plon, Nourrit et Cie, [1883]. The image was graphically edited by Lisa Yannucci.

31 Le bon roi Dagobert (The Good King Dagobert)
Many thanks to La Grande Bleue for contributing this song. **La Grande Bleue** (http://lagrandebleue.free.fr/) is a group of musicians who write songs and perform them for children.

Translated by Monique and Lisa.

Image Source: "Catalogue illustré de l'exposition des arts incohérents" (1884) by E. Bernard.

32 Le carillon de Vendôme (The Chimes of Vendôme)
Many thanks to Monique Palomares for contributing and translating this song (with Mama Lisa), for the midi and the sheet music.

33 Le coq est mort (The Rooster Is Dead)
Thanks to Monique Palomares for contributing and translating this song! Thanks to Lila Pomerantz for the drawing.

34 Le grand cerf (The Big Deer)
Many thanks to Monique Palomares for contributing and translating this rhyme (with Lisa) and for creating the midi music. Many thanks also to Sylvie Choffel for the second verse.

Image: Mama Lisa

35 Lundi matin (On Monday Morning)
Many thanks to Jade Kite for contributing this song. Translated by Lisa Yannucci and Monique Palomares.

36 Malbrough s'en va-t-en guerre (Marlborough Is Going to War)
Many thanks to Monique Palomares for contributing this song and creating the midi music! Translated by Lisa Yannucci and Monique Palomares.

The 1st illustration is from Imagerie d'Épinal Pellerin #442 (from the end of 19th century), edited and colorized by Monique Palomares.

The 2nd illustration is from CHANSONS ET RONDES ENFANTINES (1871) with some graphical editing by Lisa Yannucci.

37 Maudit sois-tu carillonneur (Curse You Bell-ringer)
Translation: Monique and Lisa

Image from "Church bells of England" (1912) by Henry Beauchamp Walters.
2nd image from "Change Ringing: An introduction to the early stages of the art of church or hand bell ringing for the use of beginners" (1872) by Charles Arthur William Troyte.
Both images were edited by Lisa Yannucci.

38 Meunier, tu dors (Miller, You're Sleeping)

Many thanks to Monique Palomares for contributing and translating this song (with Mama Lisa) and for creating the midi music.

39 Mon âne (My Donkey)
Translated by Lisa Yannucci and Monique Palomares.

Thanks to Lila Pomerantz for the drawing!

40 Mon beau sapin (My Beautiful Fir Tree)
Many thanks to Monique Palomares for contributing and translating this song (with Mama Lisa) and for creating the midi music.

41 Nous n'irons plus au bois (We'll Go to the Woods No More)
Many thanks to Monique Palomares for contributing this rhyme. Translated by Monique and Lisa.

Image: "Chansons nationales et populaires de France: accompagnées de notes historiques et littéraires", Volume 2 (1866).

42 Pirouette cacahuète (Pirouette Peanut Butter)
Many thanks to Monique Palomares for contributing this song and for the midi music. Translation by Monique and Lisa. Image compiled by Mama Lisa.

43 Pomme de reinette et pomme d'api (Pippin Apple and Lady Apple)
Many thanks to Blanca Castilla for contributing this song that she remembers from France. Thanks also to Monique Palomares for translating and recording this song, for providing the midi, the sheet music and the commentary.

Thanks to Lila for the wonderful illustration!

44 Promenons-nous dans les bois (Let's Stroll in the Woods)
Many thanks to Monique Palomares for contributing and translating this song (with Mama Lisa) and for creating the midi music.

45 Savez-vous planter les choux ? (Do You Know How to Plant Cabbage?)
Many thanks to Monique Palomares for contributing and translating this song (with Mama Lisa) and for creating the midi music.

Illustrations by Louis-Maurice Boutet de Monvel (1851-1913) from VIEILLES CHANSONS POUR LES PETITS ENFANTS: AVEC ACCOMPAGNEMENTS / de Ch. M. Widor (1844 - 1937); Illustrations Par M.B. de Monvel. Paris: E. Plon, Nourrit et Cie, [1883]. The images were graphically edited by Lisa Yannucci.

46 Sur le plancher une araignée (A Spider on the Floor)
Many thanks to Monique Palomares for contributing this rhyme and for creating the midi music. Translation by Monique and Lisa.

47 Sur le pont d'Avignon (On the Bridge of Avignon)
Many thanks to Monique Palomares for creating the midi music for this song.

The 1st illustration comes from THE BABY'S BOUQUET, A FRESH BUNCH OF RHYMES AND TUNES by Walter Crane (1878). The 2nd illustration is from CHANSONS ET RONDES ENFANTINES (1871) with a little graphical editing by Lisa Yannucci.

48 Sur le pont du Nord (On the North Bridge)
Translation: Monique Palomares and Lisa Yannucci.

49 Trois jeunes tambours (Three Young Drummers)
Many thanks to Jade Kite for contributing this song! Translated by Monique and Lisa.

Many thanks to Lila Pomerantz for the drawing.

50 Trois petits chats (Three Little Cats)
Many thanks to Manuela de Araujo Alves for sending another version of this song.

Translated by Monique and Lisa.

51 Un éléphant, ça trompe (One Elephant That Deceives)
Translation: Monique Palomares and Lisa Yannucci.

Many thanks to CM2 (5th grade) students, St-Ambreuil (71), France, school year 2008-2009 for the wonderful illustration!

52 Un éléphant se balançait (One Elephant was Swinging on a Spider Web)
Many thanks to Marie and Séverine for contributing this song. Translated by Monique and Lisa.

53 Un kilomètre à pied ça use, ça use (One Kilometer on Foot Wears Out Your Shoes for Good)
Many thanks to Florence Godineau for contributing this song. Many thanks also to Lucie Lasseel for completing the song. Thanks to Harald Meilicke for the alternate ending. Thanks to Melisa Roche for the drawing!

54 Un petit cochon (A Little Pig)
Many thanks to Monique Palomares for contributing and translating this rhyme and for creating the midi music. Thanks to Lila Pomerantz for the two illustrations!

55 Un, deux, trois, nous allons au bois (One, Two, Three, We Are Going into the Woods)
Many thanks to Aline Giuseppi of Algiers for contributing and translating this song.

56 Une poule sur un mur (A Hen on a Wall)
Many thanks to Monique Palomares for contributing and translating this rhyme and for creating the midi music.

57 Une souris verte (A Green Mouse)
Many thanks to INTER-COM Translations for contributing and translating this rhyme and to Monique Palomares for providing the alternate version and creating the midi music. Many thanks also to Sylvie Choffel for the additional usual lines and for her own lyrics.

Thanks to Monique Palomares for the illustration!

58 Vent frais, vent du matin (Fresh Wind, Morning Wind)
Many thanks to Monique Palomares for contributing this round. Translation by Lisa Yannucci and Monique Palomares.

About Mama Lisa's World

Mama Lisa's World (www.mamalisa.com) is the internet's premier destination for children's songs from around the globe and for discussions of international culture. It features thousands of traditional songs from over a hundred countries and cultures and a major collection of Mother Goose Rhymes. Mama Lisa's Blog focuses on global recipes, holiday traditions, poetry and lively conversations about childhood around the world.

About the Staff

Lisa Yannucci (Mama Lisa)
Lisa was inspired to start Mama Lisa's World in the mid 1990's, when her young son first became interested in nursery rhymes. She recorded several Mother Goose songs onto a computer and programmed them to play when he clicked a picture. He loved it and she became fascinated with the power of the internet to enrich the lives of children. She made the site public and has since used her background in languages and culture, and her talent as an illustrator, to oversee its tremendous growth.

Jason Pomerantz
Jason (Lisa's husband) has worked in magazine, book and web publishing for over twenty years. His personal projects have included several websites and podcasts. Along with his editorial contributions, he oversees the business and technical aspects of Mama Lisa's World.

Monique Palomares
Monique grew up at the crossroads of three cultures in the Occitan region of France. She is fluent in French, Spanish, English and Occitan and has a working knowledge of many other languages including Italian. Her years as a first grade teacher and her love of children and linguistics give her a unique insight into the power of music and song all over the world.

About You

Mama Lisa's World is made up of contributions from ordinary people from all over the globe. Please visit us at www.mamalisa.com and say hello! We want to hear about your childhood memories, your favorite recipes, your holidays and anything else you'd like to share about your culture.

Thank you for being part of our community!

(c) 2012 by Lisa Yannucci

Made in the USA
San Bernardino, CA
18 January 2019